Step-by-Step
OUTDOOR STONEWORK

Step-by-Step

OUTDOOR STONEWORK

Over twenty easy-to-build projects
for your patio and garden

Mike Lawrence

NEW
HOLLAND

Stonework

First published in the UK in 1994 by
New Holland (Publishers) Ltd
37 Connaught Street, London W2 2AZ

Reprinted 1994

ISBN 1 85368 180 6 (hbk)
ISBN 1 85368 262 4 (pbk)

Co-ordination and picture research: Elizabeth Whiting & Associates
Editor: John Boteler
US consultant: Derek Bradford AIA RIBA
Design: Cooper Wilson Design
Illustration: Rob Shone
Originated by Global Colour, Malaysia
Printed and bound in Singapore by Kyodo Printing Co (Pte) Ltd

The author would especially like to thank the following for their invaluable
assistance: Armatool Distributors Ltd., Black & Decker, Stanley Tools for loan of
tools for special photography, Jennifer Tetlow, stonemason, for allowing us to
photograph her at work. Marshalls, for loan of photographs and advice.

Contents

INTRODUCTION

No building material has a longer pedigree than stone; after all, the Stone Age was the first recognized period of human culture, and early man used stone not only as a source of invaluable tools but also as a building material of unparalleled strength, durability and versatility. Stone can be used as it occurs naturally, in boulders or random blocks and slabs split and shaped by the forces of nature, or it can be worked into precisely-cut blocks that slot together as snugly as jigsaw pieces. Above all, it offers the infinite variety that only a naturally-occurring material can exhibit.

The earliest use of stone as a building material was probably the casual gathering of loose-lying surface stone to form simple enclosures for defence and to pen animals. It would soon find a use as a paving material for consolidating soft ground, and by Egyptian times records show that it was being used in the design of decorative gardens as well as for the construction of the many meticulously-engineered pyramids and temples of the period. The Greeks and Romans loved their ornamental sacred groves and public gardens, and by the Middle Ages there was a strong tradition of landscape architecture that was to spread across every culture and every continent. In every case, stone was the predominant structural feature.

Today, stone is as popular as ever for creating a wide range of garden features, from the humblest carved ornament to the most elaborate walls, arches, terraces and steps. No longer are garden landscapers restricted to using just the types of stone provided by the accident of local geology; they can within reason obtain whatever type of stone is required so long as they are prepared to pay for the inevitably high transport costs of one of the densest building materials around.

With this point in mind, perhaps the most significant development as far as garden stonework is concerned has been the growing use of man-made stone products. These are formed by the

Below: *Stone lends itself to all sorts of outdoor uses, either in its natural form or as cut blocks and sculpted ornaments.*

vibration or compression of selected crushed aggregate to produce walling blocks, paving stones and even ornamental mouldings such as balusters and bird-baths. Not only is the product uniform in size and structural characteristics, unlike natural stone, and therefore easier for the amateur to work with; it is also generally both less expensive and more readily available. But it lacks something: the natural beauty and variety of stone is a quality that even the most ingenious manufacturer cannot hope to copy completely faithfully.

What to build

Whether you choose to work with natural stone or its man-made equivalent, there

arch, whether it is built as a free-standing feature or is contained within a high wall. Building one is a good test of your skill as a stonemason, and the results can provide a stunning centrepiece in any garden.

Every garden also needs hard surfaces for its occupants to walk on, and stone in its infinite variety is the perfect material to choose for patios, terraces, paths and steps. Large square or rectangular slabs can create paved areas on a grand scale, while the more informal pavers and setts are ideal both for paving smaller areas and for adding detail to larger schemes. Surface colour and texture have an important part to play here too, helping the paving to blend in well with its surroundings.

Stone is also the perfect material to choose for a whole host of other garden features. A garden pond set about with rocks, perhaps with a small cascade running into it, is not only an eye-catching garden feature in its own right; it also adds a third dimension – the restful sound of running water – to the twin delights of sight and smell. The presence of water allows you to broaden the variety of plants you can grow, and also encourages wildlife to visit the garden.

Lastly, you can use stone for a wide range of other garden projects, too, from rockeries to garden furniture. All are easy – and rewarding – to build and will enhance any garden design. You need few special skills or tools – just the vision to create the effect you want – and the time and patience to put it into practice.

Left: *Stone can be split into large slabs for paving, into medium-sized blocks for walling or into smaller setts for paving – here contrasted with rounded cobbles.*

Below: *Reconstituted regular stone slabs and blocks in the foreground contrast well with the mass of natural stone used for the rockery on the lawn.*

is a huge range of garden projects to which you can turn your hand.

Walls are an obvious first choice, and there is no finer walling material than stone. Finely-dressed blocks can be used to create the neatly-detailed formal look, while randomly-shaped pieces can be turned into the most attractive of all garden features, the dry-stone wall, with its rugged natural appearance and plethora of planting pockets. Unlike brickwork, stone always looks as though it belongs in the garden, especially when it has begun to weather, and is therefore the perfect choice for boundary walls, earth-retaining walls, even low-level planters.

Another stone feature that can look particularly fine in the garden is the

WALLS

THERE IS MORE TO ENCLOSING YOUR PROPERTY THAN SIMPLY MARKING THE BOUNDARY LINES. YOU GAIN PRIVACY FROM PRYING EYES; YOU CAN KEEP CHILDREN AND FAMILY PETS FROM STRAYING; YOU CAN CONCEAL EYESORES — IN YOUR OWN GARDEN, OR NEXT DOOR; ABOVE ALL, YOU CREATE A BACKDROP AGAINST WHICH YOUR GARDEN CAN BE DISPLAYED IN ALL ITS GLORY. NOTHING DOES THIS SO WELL AS A STONE WALL. IT IS DURABLE, NEEDS LITTLE MAIN-TENANCE IF IT IS WELL CONSTRUCTED AND CAN GREATLY ENHANCE THE LOOK OF THE HOUSE AND ITS SURROUNDINGS IF A LITTLE CARE IS PUT INTO ITS DESIGN AND CONSTRUCTION.

WALLING MATERIALS

The first stage in planning any sort of walling project is to choose your materi-als. How much choice you have often depends on where you live; country areas are likely to offer local stone in abundance, while in town you may be restricted to a selection of man-made blocks unless you are prepared to foot heavy delivery bills. Wherever you live, your primary aim should be to choose materials that complement those already used for the house, for other buildings on the site and for surfaces like paths and patios. This is particularly important as far as boundary walls are concerned if you live in an area where one local building material is predomi-nantly used.

Natural stone is without doubt the most beautiful material to use for garden walling projects, since by its very nature it looks as if it belongs in the garden. Apart from its beauty, stone is also by definition more durable than the average man-made block; after all, it has been around a long time. The most common stone walling materials are limestones, sandstones and granites; slate (shale) and flint can also be used, but are generally more difficult to work with. Colours vary from area to area, and size is really a question of pot luck. The stones themselves may be undressed (in the natural, as-quarried state), semi-dressed (cut into reasonably uniform blocks but with uneven surfaces) or fully-dressed (with square, machine-cut faces). The less dressed the stone is, the less it costs. Unless you live near quarries — which may have suit-able stone in stock — you may have trouble locating supplies; because the cost of transport is so high, you will find relatively little stone stocked by subur-ban builders' merchants in some areas or selected garden centres — what they do stock is mainly intended for rockeries — and you may have no option but to hire a lorry and drive to a quarry your-self. However, it is a good idea to check your local classified telephone directory for any local stone merchants first.

Man-made blocks come in three main types. The most popular is best described as reconstituted stone; this is made by bonding aggregates and pigments together to create blocks with one decorative face and end, in imita-tion of natural quarried stone. Blocks of this sort have the advantage that they are regular and of uniform size, making planning, estimating and building easier than using natural stone. They come in a range of sizes, colours and textures and can be laid just like bricks. In some areas they are even made as multi-stone blocks complete with recessed pointing, and are quicker to build up than individual blocks – ideal for the waller in a hurry. They are stocked by builders' merchants, garden centres and specialist stockists.

Pierced screen blocks are also formed from pressed aggregate, but instead of being solid they have cut-outs in various patterns passing through the block. They are ideal for screen walls where complete privacy is not needed, but the construction can be weak unless additional reinforcement is included. They are usually about 300 mm (12 in) square and 100 mm (4 in) thick; colours may range from white through yellow to buff or just grey. Builders' merchants, garden centres, and specialist stockists such as concrete manufacturers are the likeliest sources of supplies.

Right: *If you want walls with a completely natural look, a dry-stone structure is the perfect choice both for boundaries and for smaller feature walls. Its irregular stones provide plenty of planting pockets.*

Plain concrete blocks are not intended to be on show and are used mainly for constructing retaining walls which will then be faced with a decorative skin. The advantage of using them in this situation is their low cost and the speed with which the wall can be built up. Sizes range from 390 mm to 600 mm (16 to 24 in) long, 150 to 300 mm (6 to 12 in) high and up to 200 mm (8 in) thick. They could be used for perimeter walls and the like if finished with a mortar rendering, especially if other materials prove too expensive. Buy them from builders' merchants or concrete manufacturers.

For more details on choosing natural and man-made stone for your garden projects, please see pages 86-87.

Wall design

Once you have settled on the materials you intend to use, your next decision is what sort of wall to build. Will it be free-standing or earth-retaining? Will it be solid or pierced with openings? Will it be straight, curved or built in bays? Will it be mortared or dry-laid? What bonding pattern will be used? And how long, high and thick will it be?

You can build free-standing walls 100 mm (4 in) thick up to a height of around 450 mm (18 in) without additional support, but over this height you should incorporate a 230 mm (9 in) square pier every 3 m (10 ft). A wall 200 mm (8 in) thick can be built up to 1350 mm (4ft 6 in) high without piers. On long straight runs of mortared wall, you should aim to incorporate an unmortared movement joint every 6 m (20 ft) to prevent ground movement from cracking the wall. Earth-retaining walls should be at least 230 mm (9 in) thick unless reinforcement is incorporated in the structure. Most walls should be mortared for strength; the only exception is if the walls are built of natural stone, where the techniques of building dry-stone walls help to ensure the structure's strength and stability. Get professional advice on the wall thickness and slope if building one higher than about 1 m (3 ft).

You can create openings in stone and block walls by using an open bonding pattern. Gaps can be left in retaining walls to encourage plants to grow for a more natural look.

The wall itself does not have to be built in straight lines, and curves or bays can help to soften its impact and help it to blend in with the contours of the garden. It is often worth experimenting with dry-laid stones or blocks to get an idea of how different ideas will look, before you actually start laying foundations and building in earnest; it is easier to visualise what something will look like in the flesh than on paper.

Walls do not all have to be boundary walls; you can build them as screens to sub-divide the garden into different areas or to hide eyesores such as the compost heap. You can use them to create sheltered sitting areas facing a favourite view, while low walls can form terracing between different lawn or flower bed levels on sloping sites; they can even contain a raised ornamental pond or water garden.

Your walls can also be the perfect backdrop for plants, and because a well-built wall will need no maintenance (unlike the average fence), there is no reason why you should not grow plants up them, provided that you create suitable planting areas in front of the wall face. Such a wall can also provide screening from the prevailing winds, and if it faces the sun you will create a suntrap that will enable you to grow species that would not survive in the open. You can even grow plants within walls if you build them as a double skin and fill the centre with earth.

The only restraining factor when it comes to designing walls is your ingenuity. If you are stuck for ideas, do not forget the enormous wealth of ideas on show in public gardens or stately homes all over the country; the scale may be grander than you can manage in your own back garden, but the design principles are still the same.

Professional help

Mention was made earlier of the vital importance of building walls that are strong and safe. From time to time the news media carry stories of the collapse of garden and boundary walls, often with tragic consequences for anyone in the immediate vicinity. It is therefore wise (and may in some countries be an essential requirement of local building codes) to get professional advice from a builder or structural engineer if you are building walls taller than about 1350 mm (4ft 6in), and essential if they are earth-retaining walls. This will ensure that the dimensions and constructional techniques you propose to use will result in a wall strong enough to do its job properly for the foreseeable future. The small expense will be more than justified in terms of the peace of mind such reassurance will bring.

You may decide that such large-scale projects are beyond your skill and ability to build, and that you will employ professional help for the construction as well as for the design. It is better to accept your limitations at the beginning of the project than to start work and find that you cannot complete the job.

Left: *Solid walling blocks combine with pierced screen blocks to form a wind-break for a favourite stone seat.*

Right: *Reconstituted paving slabs and walling blocks are easier to use than natural stone for formal features.*

WALLS

DRY STONE WALLS

Dry stone walls have been a feature of the landscape for centuries, and were the obvious choice for both livestock enclosure and boundary marking in areas where stone was plentiful. A well-built dry stone wall will stand for many years, and even a tumbledown one can be quickly restored to full health.

The skill in building dry stone walls lies in the waller's ability to select the right stones and to build them up into a stable, durable and good-looking wall.

WALL STRUCTURE

Since no mortar is used in building a true dry stone wall, it has to rely on a sound foundation and careful place-

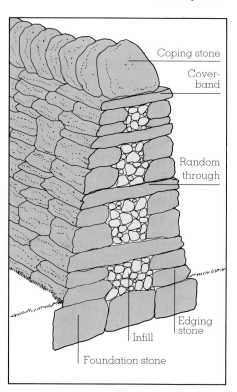

Coping stone

Cover-band

Random through

Infill

Edging stone

Foundation stone

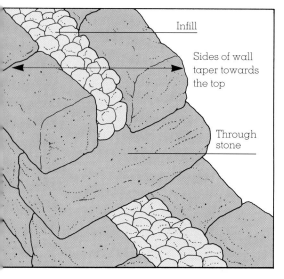

Infill

Sides of wall taper towards the top

Through stone

ment of the individual stones for its strength. At the base of the wall is a layer of large, heavy stones set in a shallow trench foundation. Above this lies the first course of the wall proper. This is built up as two separate faces, using the largest stones that are available once the foundation has been laid, to a height of about 600 mm (2 ft). The space between the two faces is filled with a 'hearting' of smaller stones, and then a course of long 'through' stones is laid so the individual stones reach from one face of the wall to the other and serve to bind them together.

Next comes a second course of facing stones, with hearting in between, a second layer of 'throughs' and, if the height of the wall requires it, a third course of facing stones and hearting.

Above and right: If the stones used are small and regular, the structure can be built up safely without the need for through stones, using a similar bonding pattern to that used for a brick wall. Coping stones complete the wall.

Above the final course of facing stones a layer of 'coverbands' is added. These project about 50 mm beyond the face of the wall, and help to bind the top course of the wall together; they also prevent rainwater from penetrating the core of the wall, and provide a firm base for the upright coping stones that finish the wall off.

The key feature of any dry stone wall is that each face of a free-standing wall slopes inwards from the foundation up

to the top. This slope is known as the 'batter', and may result in a wall being as much as 900 mm (3 ft) thick at the base and tapering to about 400 mm (16 in) at the top. On earth-retaining walls, the inner face slopes slightly backwards and the outer face has a rather steeper batter.

Walling materials

Since landowners are unlikely to take kindly to you loading up your car boot with stone from the local countryside, the chances are that you will have to buy stone for your walls from a local stonemason or quarry. He should be able to advise you on the best choice of stone; generally speaking harder, non-porous stone such as granite is ideal, but some limestones and sandstones are also suitable.

Estimating quantities is tricky – you cannot simply count the units as you can with a brick wall. Stone is generally ordered by the tonne, and you will find that one tonne will build about 1cu m (35cu ft) of wall including foundations. It is no bad thing to over-order slightly in any case; since carriage is very expensive, you do not want to have to send for a second delivery because you have run short of stone.

If you cannot find – or else cannot afford – natural stone, then the only alternative that looks anything like the real thing is broken paving stone, such as you would use for crazy paving. The broken edges are laid facing outwards so that they look reasonably natural. The one big advantage of using this

material is that the flat faces of the pieces make it easy to build the wall up evenly in courses, and you can also use slate or similar packing to avoid the appearance that the courses are too close together.

Site preparation

Make sure you have somewhere for the stone to be dumped when it is delivered, and organise helpers with wheelbarrows to transfer it to near where the wall is to be built. Then sort the stones into groups of different sizes – large foundation stones, medium-sized stones with at least one square edge for facing, long through stones and smaller infill material. It is a good idea at this stage to set aside the stones that will form the wall coping.

Apart from collecting up the tools and equipment you will need to build the wall – a spade for digging foundations, a club hammer and brick bolster for breaking the stones, a steel tape measure and a spirit level, plus gloves and stout shoes – you should also make up a batter frame to help you build the wall up to a constant and accurate slope. Make two frames from scrap battening (1) and sharpen the feet into spikes so you can set them up at opposite ends of your wall. Link them with a stringline along each face of the wall; you will move this up the frames as the wall rises.

Laying foundations

Mark out the base of the wall, and lift turf or clear surface vegetation. Then dig down to a depth of about 150 mm (6 in), or until you reach firm, undisturbed subsoil, compacting the soil by stamping or ramming it down firmly (2). In areas

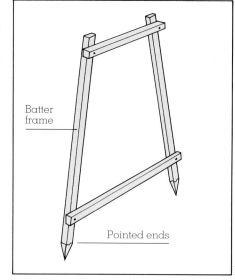

prone to prolonged frost in winter, dig even deeper – to a depth of between 450 and 600 mm (18 to 24 in).

Now you can bed in the foundation stones. These should be large and fairly flat, with the squarest edge laid at the face of the wall. Fit the stones together as best you can, and fill in gaps with smaller stones of the same thickness.

The final step before you actually start building the wall is to erect the batter frames – one at each end of the wall. Stand them alongside the foundations and use a hammer or mallet to drive their spiked ends into the ground, ready to receive their stringlines (3).

Below: Hammer small pinning stones beneath individual coping stones to ensure that they are securely bedded.

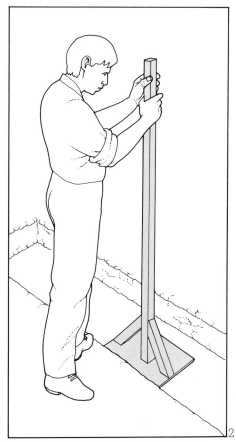

BUILDING THE WALL

Lay a course of medium-sized facing stones on the foundations along each face of the wall, again with their squarest edges facing outwards. Check with your stringline, or by 'sighting' across the batter frames, to ensure that the facing stones are set back slightly from the edges of the foundation stones. Use smaller pieces of stones to wedge the larger ones – a process called pinning – so they do not rock on the stone below. These pinning stones should always be pushed into position from the inside of the wall so they will not be seen when the wall is complete.

Pack the space between opposite faces with smaller pieces of stone, wedged as tightly as possible to ensure that the infill is well compacted and will not subside (3). Do not be tempted to use soft soil for packing; it will soon be washed out by rain, leaving the stones dangerously unstable.

Right: *A well-built dry stone wall is an object of great beauty, and need only occasional maintenance to keep it so.*

Depending on the thickness of the stone you are using, you may need to add a second or even a third course of facing stones to bring the wall height up to about 600 mm (2 ft), ready for the first course of through stones. Check that each course follows the required slope, and lay the stones so that each one overlaps a joint between the stones in the course below it (4, p15), just like stretcher bond in brickwork.

Form ends to the wall by building up a layer of long through stones at each end of the wall structure. Tie the stones into the infill at intervals with a stone laid so it projects back into the centre of the wall, and tilt the stones backwards slightly for extra stability.

Make sure that both faces and the infill are level, then lay the long through stones across the wall. They should reach from face to face for maximum strength; trim any that are over-long using your club hammer and a brick bolster. If you are short of enough stones of the right length, space those you have evenly along the length of the wall and then lay shorter 'half-throughs' between them; they should be long enough at least to reach to the centre line of the wall. Again, pin the stones inside the wall with smaller pieces of stone so they do not rock, and add infill stones in the gaps between them.

Continue building up the wall to the required height, adjusting the stringline so you keep the batter constant. A low wall may need just one more thinner layer of facing stones, followed by the layer of coverbands (the final through stones) and the coping. A taller wall (up to a maximum of about 1200 m/4 ft – higher walls may be somewhat unstable unless they are built by a specialist) will need another course of facing stones and a second layer of through

stones near the top. Complete the pinning and infilling, again checking that the top of the wall is level.

Now you can add the coverbands. These are laid so that they form a sort of damp-proof course, rather like that in a parapet wall, to prevent rain from saturating the infill. They should therefore be

laid so their facing edges project about 50 mm (2 in) beyond the batter slope, and their other edges should mesh as closely as possible with their neighbours like pieces in a jigsaw. Trim stones if necessary to get a good fit, and check that the coverband course is level. Pin any stones that are not perfectly bedded

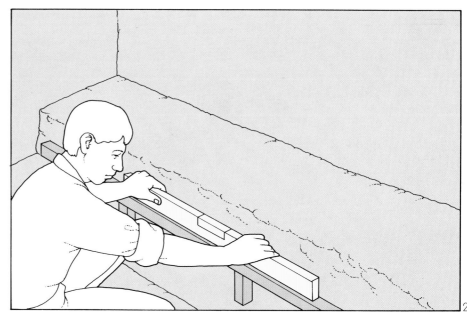

on the top course of the wall, to ensure a stable base for the coping.

If you live in an area where winters are especially severe, it is better to break with tradition and bed the coverbands in mortar. This will help reduce water penetration and subsequent frost damage – both to individual stones, and as a result of freezing forcing the stones apart and de-stabilizing the wall.

Finally, add the coping after again adjusting the stringlines (5, p16). You can use a row of evenly-matched semi-circular stones laid on edge, lay single stones flat on top of the coverband or choose the traditional buck-and-doe coping – high and low stones which are laid alternately to give an effect that resembles a line of rabbits sitting nose to tail. It is also known as cock-and-hen coping in some areas.

Whichever type you choose, set the stones closely together. With on-edge stones, set them so they all lean slightly in one direction.

EARTH-RETAINING WALLS

If you plan to build dry stone retaining walls, follow exactly the same technique as for free-standing ones using facing stones on each face of the wall and throughs at 600 mm (2 ft) intervals. You do not need a batter frame; instead build up the ends of the wall first using long through stones, and run a stringline between the two ends to act as a guide for the batter of the front face of the wall. The only difference in construction is that the inner face slopes backwards into the bank, and it is a good idea to lay the stones with a very slight backward tilt, both to improve the wall strength and to help rainwater to drain into the bank behind.

4

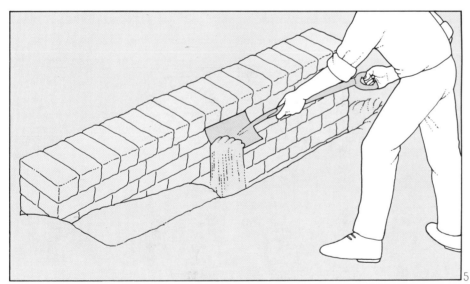

5

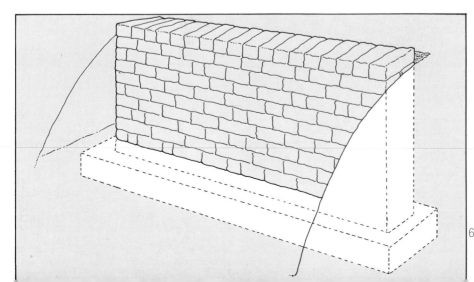

6

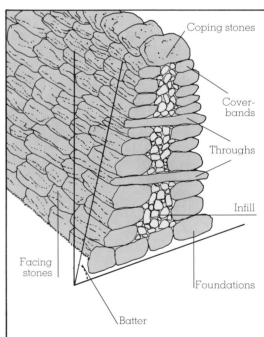

Below: *The structure of a dry-stone wall built using irregular sized stones. The most important features are the heavy foundation stones and the long through stones that bind the wall structure together. The facing stones are wedged in place with pinning stones, and the centre is filled with smaller pieces.*

Coping stones

Coverbands

Throughs

Infill

Facing stones

Foundations

Batter

Far left and left: *The first step in building a retaining wall, whether you are using random-shaped or regular stone, is to dig-out the site for the wall (1). Then check that the base on which you will be building is level (2) and add foundations for high walls. Build the wall up, using mortar to reinforce the bonding between the blocks (3), and finish off with a coping course (4). Backfill behind the wall (5) to complete the job (6).*

Raised bed wall

You can use a variation on the dry-stone walling technique to create low walls that are built to encourage an eventual clothing of plant growth. The technique is quite simple; the wall is built up using soil as the 'mortar' between the blocks, creating dozens of small planting pockets in which a variety of climbing plants can take root.

The wall can be built using either long garden walling blocks (where these are available) or pieces of broken paving slab. The former are best for a free-standing wall, with the blocks laid in two parallel rows of stretcher-bond work (end to end, with an overlap of half the block length in successive courses). Link the two halves of the wall with a header (a block laid across the two halves) after every two or three stretcher blocks.

If pieces of broken paving slab are used, the wall is best built as a cavity construction, with straight edges of slab exposed on the face of the wall and the uneven edges in its centre. The irregularities in the centre of the wall can then be filled with packed-in soil.

It must be stressed that walls built in this way should not exceed about 900 mm (3 ft) in height, and on no account should they be built as earth-retaining walls unless the blocks or slabs are set on proper concrete foundations and are bedded on mortar, with soil planting pockets only in the vertical joints.

Building the wall

Start by clearing the site, and dig a level trench to act as the footing for the wall. Compact it thoroughly with a length of fence post or similar implement, ramming pieces of broken brick or similar material into areas that are soft or have been recently disturbed. Check that the base of the trench is approximately level; any minor discrepancies can be made up by increasing or decreasing the depth of the soil bed laid beneath the first course of stones.

Build the wall up course by course, tamping each block down into a bed of loose soil about 50 mm (2 in) to compact this down to about half its thickness. This works best if the soil is slightly damp. As you complete each course, check that it is level using a long timber straightedge and a spirit level, and raise or lower any stones as necessary by adding or removing a little soil.

If you are using broken paving slabs to build the two faces of the wall, set each succeeding course back towards the wall centre by about 12 mm ($\frac{1}{2}$ in) so the face of the wall slopes very slightly inwards towards the wall centre as it rises. This will improve the stability of the wall.

Continue building the wall up course by course until it reaches the required height. Because only soil is used to bond the blocks together, it is a good idea to add mortared-on coping stones along the top of the wall to help throw rainwater clear of the wall faces and prevent it from washing out the soil. Then you can push small plant cuttings into the planting pockets.

1

2

1 Start by excavating the site for the planter, digging down until you reach firm, undisturbed subsoil.

2 Level and compact it thoroughly.

3 Build up the planter course by course, using sieved soil or peat to bed the slabs in place.

4 Check that the courses are building up truly level as the wall rises.

5 Continue adding courses, sloping the wall face backwards slightly to give the structure extra strength.

Above: This raised bed has matured over several years to become an attractive feature in an otherwise flat garden.

Moss and lichen can be encouraged by a liberal painting of natural yoghurt or pig dung diluted in water.

WALLS

REGULAR BLOCK WALLS

The main advantages of choosing blocks as the material for your garden walls are that they are comparatively inexpensive, easily obtainable, weatherproof and easy to lay because of their regular shape and size. Building a simple block wall in the garden is also the perfect way to practise your masonry skills, in readiness for some more advanced projects.

ESTIMATING QUANTITIES

Reconstituted garden walling blocks are made in a wide range of sizes. To enable you to estimate the quantities you need for a project such as building a wall, you must first decide whether you will use just one size of block, just as if you were working in brick, or whether you want to mix up a number of different sizes to create visually interesting bonding patterns. If you are using just one size it is a simple matter to estimate quantities by working out how many blocks will be needed to lay one course the length of the wall, and then to multiply this by the number of courses

required. For walls of mixed design, the best solution is to plan the bonding pattern accurately to scale on squared paper, and then to count up how many blocks of each type will be needed.

Finally, it is wise to order a few extra blocks. You may ruin some in cutting them; others may have been damaged by careless handling during delivery.

MORTAR FOR BLOCK WALLS

Mortar for building block walls is made up of cement, soft (well-graded builders') sand and either lime or a chemical plasticiser. You can mix your own mortar from separate ingredients, or buy pre-packed dry ready-mixed bricklaying mortar. The latter is probably simpler for a small job, but will be expensive for a large one. If you prefer to mix your own mortar, it is easiest to buy masonry cement, which has the plasticiser added and also comes in 50 kg (110 lb) bags, plus 0.2 cu m (about 300 kg/6 cwt) of sand for each bag of cement. For smaller bag sizes, use the same 1:6 cement:sand ratio for estimating quantities. See page 90 for more details about mixing mortar.

SITE PREPARATION

Excavate your trench to a depth of about 250 mm (10 in), ram in a 100 mm (4 in) layer of hardcore and drive in timber pegs which you can level using a

straightedge and spirit level. Then, lay the concrete, tamping it down well until it is level with the tops of the pegs, (in very cold or hot, dry weather, cover it with polythene to maintain its moisture content), and leave it to harden for two or three days. Do not worry about getting a perfectly smooth surface; the first mortar course can take up any slight irregularities. If frost threatens, it is best to postpone the concreting until warmer weather is promised. See page 14 for more details about setting out wall foundations.

BUILDING THE WALL

1 Before laying any blocks, it is a good idea to dry-lay the first course on the foundation strip, with a 10 mm (1/2 in) gap between each block, so you can work out the precise position of end piers and corners. Then you can spread a bed of mortar on the concrete, ready to receive the first course of blocks.
2 To keep your wall straight, you should set up stringlines between pegs driven into the ground at each end of the wall. Then butter some mortar onto one end of the first block and set it in place at one end of the wall, with its face in line with the stringline. If the wall starts with a pier, lay the first block at right angles to the stringline.
3 Repeat this buttering and laying for subsequent blocks, continuing until you reach the end of the wall or the first

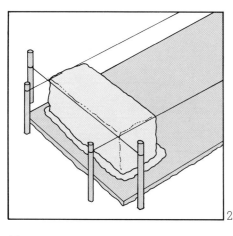

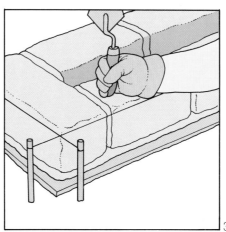

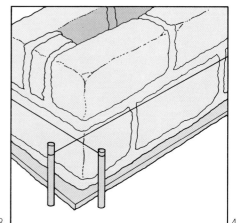

1

3

4

2

5

corner. At intermediate piers, lay two blocks side by side, end on to the face of the wall. Then go back and check that all the blocks are in line with the string-line, and are sitting level with each other; tamp down any that are high, and use your spirit level to check that the whole course is truly level. Trim off excess mortar from the joints, leaving it flush with the block faces for now.

4 Now you can start the second course. The blocks are staggered in a pattern called bonding to give the wall strength. On a wall one block thick, a simple overlap known as stretcher bond is used. At the end pier, lay a whole block as shown, and complete the second course of the pier with a half-block. Then continue laying the second course; note that at intermediate piers cut blocks are centred over the two end-on blocks in the first course to maintain the bonding.

5 The third course is laid out in identical fashion to the first, and the fourth is the same as the second. Simply continue building up the wall in this way, check-ing that each course is level and that the wall is rising truly vertically. It's a good idea to make up a gauge rod from a length of timber, marked off with alter-nate 65 mm (2^1/$_2$ in) and 10 mm (^{1}/$_2$ in) lines, so you can check that your mortar courses are even. Finish off the top of the wall with a course of coping stones, and set capping stones on top of piers.

6 On a small wall, you can leave the pointing – the neatening of the joints – until the end. On larger projects, point after every three or four courses have been completed. The simplest finish is achieved by drawing a length of rounded stick along the joints to give them a recessed rounded profile. An alternative is the struck joint, formed by drawing the pointing trowel along each joint at a slight angle. Finally, brush off excess mortar from the block surfaces with a stiff brush, and cover it with poly-thene sheeting if rain or frost threatens.

6

Right: The completed wall, pointed and finished off with irregular coping stones set on edge, looks massively solid.

WALLS

SCREEN BLOCK WALLS

Pierced screen walling blocks are available in a range of different designs, and can be used as an attractive alternative to solid masonry blocks, especially where you want an open-screen effect. You can use them on their own in conjunction with special matching pier blocks, coping stones and pier caps where available, or include them as decorative infill panels in walls built of other materials.

There is one big difference between screen walling blocks and other walling units. Because they are square there is no horizontal bonding between the walling units as the wall is built; instead they are simply stacked up in uniform vertical columns. This so-called stack bonding is naturally weak, and if you are building a complete wall with these blocks you have to incorporate piers (ideally built using special grooved pier blocks, although these may not be available in your area) in the wall structure at a maximum of 3 m (10 ft) intervals, as well as at the wall ends and at any corners. If the wall is more than two blocks high you should also use horizontal reinforcement in the form of expanding metal mesh strips to tie wall

and pier together after every two courses of blocks (which coincides in height with three pier blocks). The mesh strips should also be used between every course along the length of the wall.

To give the whole structure additional strength and rigidity, reinforcement can also be used within the hollow piers, in the form of 16 mm (¾ in) diameter steel rod or 50 mm (2 in) square angle iron, set in the foundation strip at each pier position. The piers are then filled with concrete as they rise.

BUILDING THE WALL

1 Start by marking out the position of the wall. Unless you are building on an existing concrete base slab, excavate the trench and pour the concrete for the foundation strip to finish at ground level.

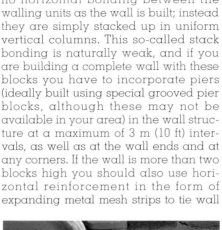

8

7

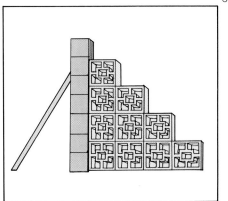

If reinforcement is being used for the piers, set the steel rods in place in the concrete at each pier position and prop them upright while it sets (see below).

2 Then build up the first pier to the required height, checking with a spirit level as you work that the pier is rising truly vertically.

3 With the pier complete, lay a bed of mortar along the foundation strip or slab and position the first walling block in the pier's side groove after buttering mortar onto its edge. Check that it sits level and square.

4 Butter more mortar onto its other vertical edge. Use a fairly soft mortar mix which will adhere easily.

5 Add a second block next to the first and check that both are level and in line. Neaten the mortar joints with your trowel.

6 Complete the rest of the first course, using your spirit level to check that the blocks are level and also that they are in line across the face of the wall.

7 Carry on adding subsequent courses to the wall in the same way. If you are building higher than two courses, use expanded metal mesh as reinforcement between the courses. Then add two more courses and leave the mortar to harden overnight. Complete the remaining courses the next day and add coping stones and pier caps.

8 If you prefer recessed pointing, use a shaping tool to form the joint shape while the mortar is still soft.

Racking back is a technique needed when working on a large project. If you are building a second wall from one of

your piers but won't finish it in one day, 'rack back' the corner to leave a stronger bond (see above).

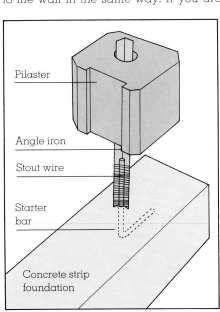

Pilaster

Angle iron

Stout wire

Starter bar

Concrete strip foundation

ARCHES HAVE BEEN USED TO BRIDGE OPENINGS IN WALLS FOR THOUSANDS OF YEARS, AND MEDIEVAL BRICKLAYERS AND STONEMASONS DEVELOPED A WIDE RANGE OF VARIATIONS ON THE BASIC SEMI-CIRCULAR ARCH THAT ARE STILL IN USE TODAY. IN THE GARDEN, AN ARCH CAN FRAME A GATEWAY, FORM AN ATTRACTIVE DIVIDER BETWEEN DIFFERENT PARTS OF THE GARDEN AND CAN EVEN PROVIDE VIEWING PORTS IN BOUNDARY WALLS. THE CONSTRUCTION TECHNIQUE IS MUCH THE SAME IN EVERY CASE.

The secret of successful arch building lies in ensuring that the arch is strong enough to support its own weight, and that the masonry below and beside it can withstand the outward thrust which the arch transmits to it. Building an arch into a run of wall ensures that the second point is safely dealt with, and accurate setting-out of the stones or

Left: Smaller arches can be safely built using randomly-shaped stones so long as they are well bedded in mortar.

man-made blocks that will form the arch takes care of the first.

PLANNING THE ARCH

While it is possible to form an arch in a wall one block thick (in other words, a wall built in stretcher bond), such a construction is not really strong enough for a full-height gateway. Any wall of this height should be built in 230 mm (9 in) thick masonry.

The arch itself is then formed of a semi-circle of blocks laid so that their ends (the

Above: *You can also build arches in garden walls, continuing the wall structure above and to either side of the opening.*

Left: *A large arch such as this is best built with closely-fitting dressed stones forming the arch itself.*

headers) are exposed on each face of the wall. For a typical domestic garden arch 1 to 1.2 m (3 to 4 ft) wide, the arch shape is formed by setting the blocks so that they almost touch, filling the gaps between them with wedge-shaped fillets of mortar. If the upper curve of the arch is to be left exposed, it is usual to lay two (or even

three) rows of blocks to give the arch both necessary strength and pleasing proportions. However, if the arch is to be surrounded by masonry a single row of blocks can be used. In this case you will need to do some careful cutting of the blocks that will abut the upper surface of the arch to create a neat finish.

You are not restricted to building semi-circular arches, although these tend to look the most pleasing in a garden setting. An alternative is the so-called segmental arch, which is just a smaller part of the circumference of a larger circle. Here again, careful cutting of the surrounding blockwork will be called for.

FREESTANDING ARCHES

If you plan to finish off an opening in a garden wall with an arch, the first step is to build up the wall in blockwork to the level at which the arch will start – known as the springing point. This is usually at between 1.5 and 1.8 m (5 to 6 ft)

above ground level, to allow ample headroom beneath the centre of the arch. Make sure that the coursing at each side of the opening is level, otherwise the arch will start its life lopsided and will always look unsymmetrical. As mentioned earlier, the ideal pier separation is likely to be between 1 and 1.2 m (3 to 3½ ft); if you intend hanging a gate within the opening, measure its width carefully (including the hinges and fastenings) and leave the appropriate gap between the piers.

MAKING AN ARCH FORMER

The first step in constructing the arch itself is to make up a former to support

the arch blockwork while you lay it. Measure the pier separation carefully, divide the figure by 2 to get the radius of the curve and draw out two semi-circles to this radius on plywood or chipboard (particle board). The simplest method of doing this is to use a makeshift compass – a pencil, a piece of string and a nail.

Cut out the semi-circles with a jigsaw (sabre saw) or padsaw. Then cut another piece of board or softwood so its length matches the arch diameter and its width is just less than the wall thickness minus the combined thicknesses of the semi-circular former sides. Nail the two semi-circles to this.

Cut timber spacers to the same width as the base of the former, and nail these in place at intervals round the curved edge of the former to keep it rigid.

Prepare two props of scrap timber just less than the height of the piers, stand them in position and knock a brace in between them to keep them pressed against the blockwork. Lift the former into position, and check that it is level with the top of the piers and has vertical faces. Nail down through its base into the top of the props to hold it securely in place.

BUILDING THE ARCH

You can now lay the first block at each side of the arch, setting it on a wedge-shaped mortar bed so that the stretcher face which will form the underside of the arch is firmly pressed against the former.

Mark a true vertical line on the face of the former, passing through the centre of the semi-circle, and position a block (without mortar at this stage) on the centre point at the top of the former. This will form the 'keystone' of the arch.

Use another block and a pencil to mark how many whole blocks will fit in each quarter-circle between the keystone and the first block laid. Remember to allow for the thickness of the mortar joint, which should be as thin as possible at the point where the blocks will rest on the former.

Now start building up the arch, laying one block at a time at each side and adjusting the thickness of the mortar as necessary so the blocks line up with your pencil marks. Carry on until you reach the keystone position; then butter some mortar onto each face of the last block, and gently tap it into place. If you find that the keystone will not fit and you cannot reduce the spacing of the other blocks, either trim the keystone down slightly with a bolster or an angle grinder, or use slips of roof or quarry tile instead to form the keystone.

With the ring complete, use a timber straightedge to check that the face of the ring is flat and in line with the face of the blockwork at each side of the opening. Point up the joints between the blocks on each face of the arch. Then spread a bed of mortar about 10 mm (1/2 in) thick over the upper surface of the arch, ready for the second row of blocks.

Lay these as for the first course, trying to prevent too many of the joints from coinciding with those in the inner ring by adjusting the thickness of the mortar wedges. You should aim to finish the ring with two blocks sitting either side of the arch centre line, above the keystone in the first ring.

Point the joints on the face and top surface of the second ring, and leave everything to harden for at least 48 hours. Then carefully remove the props and let the former drop down out of the way. Trim away any excess mortar from the underside of the arch and neaten the pointing there.

BUILT-IN ARCHES

If you decide to continue the wall upwards so that the arch will be completely surrounded by masonry, simply continue laying courses of blocks on top of the existing wall at each side. In each course, cut the block that will abut the arch so it will match the angle of the ring at that point, allowing for a 10 mm (½ in) thick mortar joint all round the curve. For the neatest possible effect, use a small angle grinder to cut these blocks to the precise angle required.

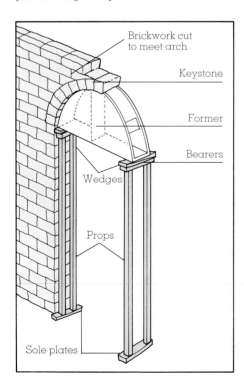

Brickwork cut to meet arch
Keystone
Former
Bearers
Wedges
Props
Sole plates

Patios

If you are about to start work on creating a new patio — or even renovating or extending your existing one — some careful planning will not only help you to make the best possible use of the site; it will also help the job to proceed in an orderly fashion and with the minimum of disruption. This planning not only covers your choice of site and materials; it also enables you to deal with obstacles such as trees and manholes.

The idea of having a hard-surfaced area in the garden on which to set your garden furniture, sunbathe, have a barbecue or create a playground for the children is a fairly recent one in countries with a cool climate. Even the word is imported – it's Spanish, and originally described a roofless courtyard.

Until the patio's import from sunnier climes, the grander sort of home had a terrace on which to walk and admire the view, while humbler abodes had a simple back yard which was little used for leisure purposes. But all that has changed now, and no self-respecting home is complete without its patio.

First Thoughts

If you are planning a new patio, the first thing to do is to sit down and work out exactly what you expect it to do for you. Will it be used mainly as an outdoor room when the weather is fine, with chairs and a table where you can sit and read, sunbathe, eat and entertain friends? If so, will you want to include features such as a barbecue? Will the furniture be movable or built-in as part of the patio construction? Will you need space so that the children have somewhere to play when the lawn is wet? Do you want to include a washing line, so you don't have to trudge down the garden on winter days? Answers to all these questions will help you to envisage exactly what sort of patio you want, in terms of both its size and its features.

Patio Materials

At this stage it is also a good idea to start thinking about the sort of materials you want to use for your patio, since this will have a direct bearing on your design and planning. The choice is between plain concrete, paving slabs of natural or reconstituted stone, and bricks or block pavers.

Concrete is comparatively inexpensive, and can obviously be used to create a patio of any shape or size, however unusual. Its drawbacks are that the surface is visually pretty uninspiring (although a variety of textured surface finishes can be created), and it is hard work to lay, even if you do order it ready-mixed. You will need quite a lot of site preparation, plus formwork to contain the concrete as it is poured. However, it makes the most durable patio surface if it is well laid, and can always be treated as a sound base for more decorative surface materials.

Paving slabs are the most popular choice for patio surfaces. They are available in a wide range of types, shapes and sizes. Natural stone slabs are an ideal choice if you are near a quarry or other local source of supply, but if you are not they are likely to be expensive because of haulage costs. Man-made slabs, though, are relatively inexpensive and are widely available from local DIY superstores, garden centres, builders' merchants or specialist suppliers. There are squares and rectangles in a variety of sizes, colours and surface textures – including some very good imitations of natural split stone – which allow you to experiment with layouts more exciting than the traditional chequerboard or stretcher-bond arrangements. You can also buy inter-locking hexagons, and even round stones that can be intermingled with materials such as cobbles. Laying is easy – either on a sand bed or on mortar over an existing concrete base – but larger slabs can be heavy to handle. The biggest advantage of slabs over other materials is the speed with which you can lay even a substantial patio and have it ready for use. The one

Left: *Patio surfaces can complement or contrast with the materials used for the house. Here, slate set in mortar is the perfect foil for the house brickwork.*

The solution is to look elsewhere.

For example, by siting it at one side of the garden you will be able to avoid the shadow of the house, and putting it at the bottom of the garden could give you a whole new view of your property. Think too about privacy, especially if you are an ardent sunbather; picking a site that is not too overlooked will do wonders for your peace of mind!

If you're lucky enough to have a flat garden, the actual patio construction will be a strictly two-dimensional affair, but if the land slopes up, down or across your patio site you will have some heavier work to do – excavation, back-filling (or a combination of the two), plus building some earth retaining walls to keep patio and garden apart.

If the patio is to adjoin the house, you have to make sure that its finished surface will be at least 150 mm (6 in) below the level of the house damp course to avoid heavy rain splashing back above it and causing damp penetration. If the garden slopes steeply away from the house, you may be able to minimise the amount of backfilling involved by having the patio level well below the DPC, and reaching it by steps from the house. But if the garden slopes up from the house, you need to think about drainage from the patio surface; otherwise your enclosed low-level patio will turn into a pond in wet weather.

Lastly, once you have decided where your patio will be sited and how big it will be, it is time to look at whether there are any obstacles in the way of your plans – things like manholes (which can often be disguised), mature trees (which you may be able to make into a feature of the patio), even existing structures such as paths, steps and clothes lines.

MAKING DETAILED PLANS

For all but the simplest rectangle it pays to make a scale drawing of your proposals before you start the actual construction. This allows you to estimate materials accurately and also to work out precisely how you will overcome any site obstacles.

Work on squared paper to a scale of, say, 1:20 – this means that every 10 mm on your drawing represents 200 mm on the site. If you prefer to work in imperial measurements, use a scale of 1:24 – 1 in on the plan equals 2 ft on the ground. Measure up the site carefully so you can draw existing features onto the plan. If the site slopes and excavation and retaining walls will be needed, measure the falls carefully so you can produce

---

disadvantage is that it is tricky to lay them in shapes other than rectangles unless you are prepared for a lot of cutting to shape.

Block pavers are a comparatively recent arrival on the DIY scene in certain countries, although they have been used in public works for years. They are roughly brick-sized, so they are easy to handle, and come in a range of colours and textures. Most are simple rectangles, but there are also inter-locking shapes which can look very attractive over small areas. They are designed to be laid over a sand bed with no mortar joints, so they can be placed and levelled very quickly (and taken up again if necessary). Because of their small size, they can also cope with curves and other unusual shapes far

more readily than slabs.

To get an idea of what is available in your area, visit local suppliers – DIY superstores, garden centres, builders' merchants or concrete manufacturers – so you can see colours and textures 'in the flesh' before making your choice.

CHOOSING A SITE

The next thing you should do is decide where the patio is going to go. Nine times out of ten, the automatic choice is to put it across the back of the house, where it acts as a sort of stepping stone between house and garden. However, unless your house faces broadly to the south in the northern hemisphere, or north in the southern hemisphere, you will not get much sun by siting it here.

PATIOS

sectional drawings as well to indicate the precise positions of steps, walls and other three-dimensional features.

If you are intending to use paving slabs, it makes sense to minimise the amount of cutting you have to do by sizing the patio so that, if possible, it consists of rows of whole slabs. This means that you need to know the size of the slabs. Most are 450 or 600 mm (18 or 24 in) across, but some ranges include half-slabs too to finish rows and, with square slabs, to enable you to stagger joints in alternate rows if you want to. With concrete and block pavers, you obviously have far greater flexibility – a concrete patio can be any size or shape you want, and block pavers are small enough for cutting not to be a major problem.

Now you can draw in the outline of the patio and add details of any other features such as walls, steps, planters and the like that you want to incorporate into it. With paving slabs, you can even draw in the individual slabs – useful for estimating quantities, as well as giving you a chance to alter the laying pattern so you can cope with obstacles such as manholes without having to do too much awkward cutting. If you are planning to lay slabs with different textures or colours to create a pattern, now is the time to colour these in – again both to help accurate estimating and to act as a guide when you start laying the slabs.

COPING WITH MANHOLES

Manholes are one of the most common obstacles when it comes to laying a patio. They are unsightly things at the best of times, and the temptation is simply to pave over them. While frowned on by professionals (and some regional authorities), this is acceptable so long as you take steps to prevent soil or sand from entering the drains and are prepared to lift the paving materials in the event of a blocked drain occurring. This means sticking to loose-laid materials – slabs or block pavers – on a sand bed (and remembering to tell your purchaser what you have done if you ever move house).

As a precaution against sand finding its way into the chamber, you should cover the manhole with a sheet of heavy-duty polythene sheeting, laid so it extends about 150 mm (6 in) beyond the chamber all round. It is also worth giving the manhole cover a generous coat of proprietary rustproofer before covering it up, especially if it is one of the lightweight galvanised types rather

1

2

3

RENOVATING AN OLD PATIO

If you inherit an old and run-down garden, you may be fortunate enough to discover an overgrown and derelict area of paving. A mess it may be: however, the one thing that has probably survived intact is the paving itself, and by clearing the area and then lifting and re-laying the old slabs you will be able to create a new patio with all the charm of weathered stone, and at a fraction of the cost.

1 Start by clearing the area of weeds and other foliage that has encroached on it.
2 Working from the edge of the paved area, start lifting individual stones and breaking up any old mortar pointing.
3 If the subsoil is well compacted, re-lay the slabs on pats of mortar. Otherwise use a 50 mm (2 in) thick sand bed.
4 Use square-edged pieces to form the new edge of the re-laid patio.
5 Complete the renovation by re-point-ing all the gaps between the stones.

4

5

than solid cast iron.

Obviously, you cannot do this if you are laying concrete or bedding slabs or crazy paving in mortar. Here there is no alternative but to build up the walls of the chamber so that the cover will finish flush with the patio surface. You can always disguise its presence by standing a planter on top of it.

PROVIDING DRAINAGE

Any 'solid' patio should have a slight slope to stop rainwater from forming puddles on the surface, although this is not critical with slabs and pavers laid loose over a sand bed because water can drain away through the open joints. For a patio adjoining the house wall, the slope should obviously be away from the house. Where the patio will be a sunken affair in a sloping garden, you should also incorporate a surface gully at some point near the centre of the patio area and link it to a drain running to a soakaway. You are generally not allowed to drain surface water into an existing foul water drain or sewerage system.

Left and below: *Reclaimed paving stones have the attractive patina of age that modern paving materials can take years of natural weathering to acquire.*

Left: *Instead of pointing between the stones, fill the gaps with soil and plant them to encourage spreading ground cover.*

PATIOS

WORKING ROUND TREES

If you have a mature tree within the area your patio will occupy, aim to lay your paving material no closer to it than about three times the trunk diameter. This will ensure that the tree is not starved of water and will prevent subsequent growth from disturbing the paving materials. With slabs and pavers, set those round the opening on a mortar bed to prevent them from shifting and to form a neat edge.

USING EXISTING BASES

You can generally resurface existing concrete patios by laying slabs or block pavers on top of them so long as raising the surface level by up to 100 mm (4 in) will not cause damp problems in an adjoining house wall. If the concrete is badly cracked, aim to lay your new surface loose on a sand bed; otherwise so long as it is in reasonably sound condition you can use a mortar bed instead and then point up any of the

joints which occur between the slabs.

If you want to extend an existing area of concrete, the weak spot will be the joint between old and new areas. Break up the edge of the existing area and brush on a liberal dose of PVA or latex bonding agent to ensure a strong bond at this point.

LAYING A PATIO

Laying a patio is one of the simplest and most satisfying outdoor construction projects you can tackle, and is a golden opportunity to get the hang of some basic building techniques too. The actual job does not need a great deal of skill, just your time and effort, both of which are effectively free. Here is how to lay a patio using paving slabs, first on sand and then on mortar; block pavers are covered on page 36.

PREPARING THE BASE

Unless you are planning to use crazy paving, you will get perfectly satisfactory results by laying your slabs on a

sand base about 30 mm to 50 mm (1 in to 2 in) thick: no mortar is needed. However, this base must be flat, with a slight slope away from the house for drainage, and must be properly prepared if you are to avoid subsidence in the future. Most importantly of all, it must not be built up in such a way that the damp–proof course (DPC) in the house wall is bridged. Ideally, the finished patio surface should be about 150 mm (6 in) below DPC level, to prevent heavy rain from splashing back up the wall and causing damp penetration.

This means you will probably have to do some excavation of the patio site, even if only to remove vegetation from the area. If the subsoil is firm, do not disturb it; however, if it is at all loose, you will have to excavate to a depth of about 150 mm (6 in) and lay a 100 mm (4 in) layer of well-rammed hardcore. In this case it is then better to lay slabs on a mortar bed rather than on sand.

You can of course also lay new slabs over an existing surface – concrete, for example – so long as the finished patio surface will still be at least 150 mm (6 in) below the level of the house damp course.

ESTIMATING QUANTITIES

With square or rectangular slabs laid in rows, working out how many you require is quite straightforward so long as you know how big the slabs are; you will need x rows, each containing y slabs – a total of x times y slabs in all. Order a few extra slabs to allow for unforeseen breakages.

Sand is sold by the cubic metre or cubic yard and parts thereof, so to work out how much you will need measure the patio area in square metres and divide the answer by 20 to get the volume required. For example, a patio 8 m (about 26 ft) wide and 5 m (16 ft) deep would need 2 cu m of sand. Order it from your local builders' merchant or transport company, who should be able to deliver hardcore too if you need it.

LAYING SLABS ON MORTAR

Start by dry-laying the slabs you are using so you can work out where cut slabs will be needed. Then mark your starting point clearly, lift the slabs and the turf and excavate to a depth of about 150 mm (6 in) to expose solid, undisturbed sub-soil. Then shovel in a 100 mm (4 in) thick layer of broken brick or coarse aggregate and ram it down thoroughly to consolidate it. If you are laying your patio over existing concrete, simply

Right: *The finished patio has a smooth surface that is good-looking, practical and also easy to keep clean.*

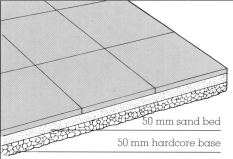
1 A typical patio cross-section – slabs laid on sand or mortar over hardcore.
50 mm sand bed
50 mm hardcore base

2 Excavate soft subsoil, then tip in a layer of hardcore about 50 mm (2 in) thick.

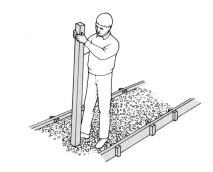
3 Tamp the hardcore down well into the subsoil with a heavy baulk of timber.

4 Check that the hardcore is level by drawing a batten across its surface.

sweep the surface clean and remove any loose concrete, ready to receive the new slabs.

You can lay the slabs in a continuous mortar bed, but this increases both the cost of the job and the amount of mortar you will have to mix. Instead, either put down five dabs of mortar, one under each corner of the slab and one under the middle, or lay a narrow band of mortar beneath the perimeter of the slab plus, again, one in the centre.

Bed the first slab on the mortar and tamp it down firmly with the handle of your club hammer.

Use your spirit level to check that the slab is level in one direction and that it has a slight fall in the other – away from the house if the patio adjoins it. The degree of fall is not critical; the bubble on the spirit level should be just off-centre in the direction of the slope.

Lay subsequent slabs in the same way, butting them tightly up against their neighbours as you work and checking the levels continuously. If a slab is lying too low, lift it and add some more mortar before tamping it back. Use spacers for even joints.

Cut and fit slabs as necessary to complete the paved area, laying them in the same way as the whole ones. Make sure that edge slabs have a continuous mortar bed beneath them, and finish it off neatly with your trowel. Then mix up some fairly dry mortar to use for pointing the joints.

Fill gaps with mortar if they are too narrow for a cut slab.

To point the joints, cut a sausage-shaped portion of mortar, lay it along the joint and use the edge of your trowel to chop it down into the gap. Alternatively, use an offcut of thin board such as hardboard held on edge to press the mortar down. Finish the joint neatly, then move onto the next one. Leave mortar droppings on the slab surfaces to dry, then brush them off; if

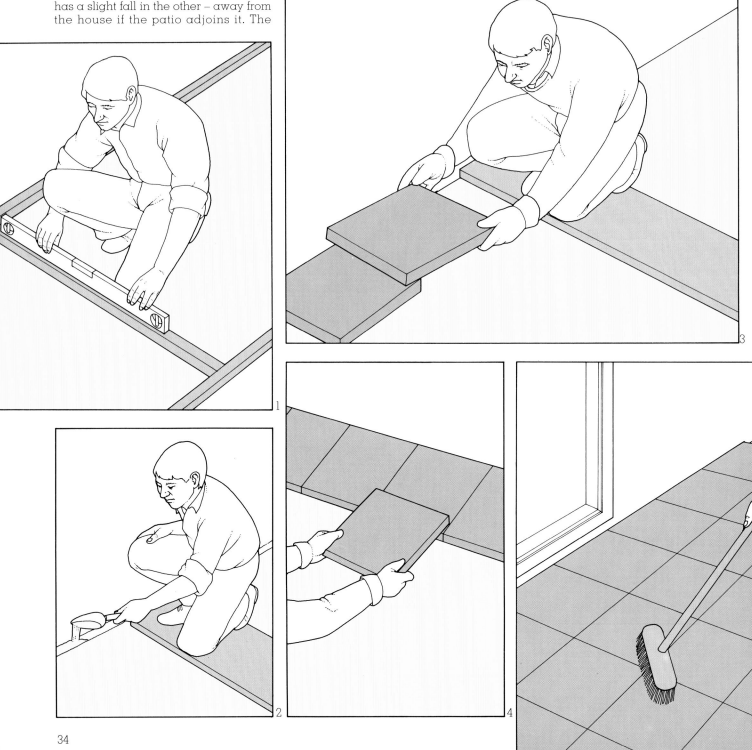

you try to remove them while they are still wet, they will stain the surface.

LAYING SLABS ON SAND

1 Begin by marking out the patio area accurately, either by dry-laying slabs or by using pegs and stringlines. Then excavate as necessary – see PREPARING THE BASE – and check that the subsoil or hardcore is roughly level. Its surface should be about 90 mm (3 in) below the surrounding ground level, so that once the sand bed and the slabs are laid the patio surface will be at the same level as the surrounding ground; actually, it is better to aim for it to be fractionally lower, so you can run your mower along the lawn edge without touching the paving.

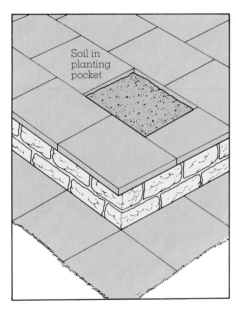
Soil in planting pocket

Save topsoil for use elsewhere in the garden; if you have to excavate a lot of subsoil, either use it to create a raised feature elsewhere in the garden, or else hire a mini-skip and have it taken away. If you are worried about weed growth, treat the patio area with a liberal dose of long-acting weedkiller at this stage.

To make it easier to get the sand bed the right depth, place 50 mm (2 in) square battens at intervals across the area to be paved. Then tip and rake out the sand between them and use a long plank spanning the battens to level it.

2 Once you have got a firm, level sand bed, lift the battens and fill in the gaps left behind with more sand.

3 Now all you have to do is to lay the slabs. Start at the edge next to the house wall, kneeling on a plank so you do not disturb the sand bed unduly, and bed the first row in place. As you work, check that each slab is level with its neighbour, scooping out or adding sand as necessary, and tamp the slab down gently but firmly with the handle of a club hammer or an offcut of heavy timber – a piece of fence post, for example.

4 Lay subsequent rows in the same way, sliding each slab into position off the edge of its neighbour in the preceding row rather than standing it on edge and then lowering it to a horizontal position. Aim for closely-butted joints, and check

the alignment of the rows as you work.

If you have to cut the occasional slab, mark the cutting line with chalk and then cut a groove along the line with a brick bolster and club hammer. A few firmer blows on the line should result in a clean break along it. If you have a lot of slabs to cut, it is worth hiring a power tool called an angle grinder, which will both do the job quickly and more accurately and will also save a lot of effort and broken slabs!

5 With all the slabs laid, all you need to do now is brush some sand and sieved soil into the joints. If the perimeter of the patio will be above the level of the surrounding ground, you need some form of edge restraint to prevent the border slabs from creeping outwards. This can be provided by bedding bricks or garden walling blocks round the edge of the patio on a mortar bed, or by using lengths of preservative-treated timber – say 75 x 25 mm (3 x 1 in) in cross-section – set on edge and held in place with stout pegs driven into the ground.

Your newly-laid patio will need little in the way of maintenance. An occasional watering with weedkiller will stop weeds from growing along the soil-filled joints. If any individual slabs show signs of subsidence, simply lift them with your brick bolster and sprinkle a little more sand underneath to restore them to their original level.

Patios

Laying block paving

There are two distinct forms of block paving. The first involves bedding small but regularly-shaped stone blocks known as setts in a layer of mortar, and then pointing between them. The second uses uniformly-shaped, man-made pavers which are laid on a dry sand bed and are butt-jointed closely together (1). Dry sand is then brushed into the narrow joints to lock the blocks together.

Setts, usually of granite, have been a popular surface for centuries; indeed, the cobbled streets of medieval towns were just as likely to be paved with roughly-dressed square setts as with rounded cobbles. They are immensely durable, but laying them is a highly labour-intensive process.

Block paving has not been around for nearly so long. It first became popular some twenty years ago for use in public open spaces such as shopping precincts, and then spread to the new housing market before being discovered and taken up by the DIY market. The blocks are relatively small and manageable, unlike paving slabs, and are quick and easy to lay. They are available in a wide range of colours from buff to black, and are a standard size. Their one drawback is that since the blocks are laid on a sand bed, you need to provide some form of edging all round any paved areas – even where they abut turf – to

prevent the sand from leaching away and causing the edges of the paving to spread and subside.

Interlocking pavers

Mark out, excavate and consolidate the area as for any paving project. The depth you need is 20–50 mm (¾–2 in) plus the thickness of the pavers themselves – typically around 65 mm (2⅛ in).

Next, position the edge restraints all round the area to be paved. You can use proprietary path kerbstones, a row of the pavers laid end to end or side by side, both bedded in concrete, or even preservative-treated timber planks secured with stout pegs. As you position the edging, check that each unit is accurately aligned and that opposite sides of square or rectangular sites are truly parallel to each other. If you are setting the edging in concrete, keep this at least 65 mm (2½ in) below the top surface of the edging to allow the sand bed to be laid right up to it.

When the concrete has hardened, lay the sand bed across the site and use a notched batten to level it to the required depth below the edge restraints. Then you can start laying the first pavers.

Right: *Small stone setts are ideal for paving this walled garden. Leaving small areas unpaved allows shrubs and small trees to be planted to soften the garden's appearance.*

If you are working with a pattern that runs parallel to the edging, simply build it up by working across the area row by row. Set stringlines to guide you if you are working with diagonal patterns. Tamp each paver down firmly into the sand bed with a club hammer, and check that it sits level with its neighbours.

When all the whole pavers have been laid, split and fit any cut pieces that are needed to complete the pattern. It is advisable to hire a hydraulic block splitter if you have a lot of cutting to do; otherwise, you could use a brick bolster and club hammer. Finish off by brushing sand into the joints, then sweep the finished surface.

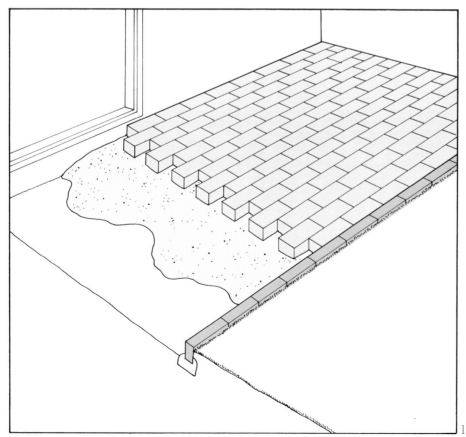

1

Above: To create a stone mosaic as a feature within a larger area of paving, start by cutting a supply of roughly square stone blocks. Then bed them in soil or mortar, building up the design you want with blocks in contrasting colours. Finish off by brushing soil or dry mortar into all the joints.

LAYING SETTS

Start by excavating the site for the setts to a depth of 25 mm (1 in) more than the average thickness of the stones you are using. Consolidate any soft areas with broken brick or coarse aggregate.

Define the edge of the area that is to be paved, and spread a layer of fairly dry mortar to a depth of about 20 mm to 50 mm (1 in to 2 in) over an area of about 1 sq m (10 sq ft). Then position the row of setts that will form the edge of the area, spacing them about 12 mm (½ in) apart. Tamp them down into the mortar bed and use a timber straightedge to ensure that the tops of the setts are level with each other (2).

Carry on laying setts in rows until you have covered the first area of mortar bed. Then spread further small areas of mortar and carry on placing and levelling setts as before until the paving is complete. Leave the mortar to set hard for 48 hours.

Pointing between the setts in the traditional manner would be impossibly time-consuming and agonisingly back-breaking. The easiest way of pointing them is to make up an almost-dry mortar mix and to brush it into the joints with a stiff broom, using the bristles to tamp the mix down between the stones. Brush off any excess mortar, then spray the whole area very lightly with water from a garden hose to dampen the mortar and help it to set hard.

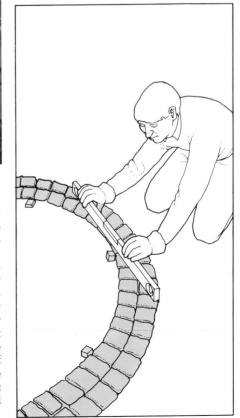

PATHS

PATHS ARE VITAL COMPONENTS OF GARDEN DESIGN, PROVIDING LINKS BETWEEN VARIOUS PARTS OF THE GARDEN THAT NOT ONLY CARRY TRAFFIC OF VARIOUS SORTS — THE MEANDERING ADMIRER OF HERBACEOUS BORDERS, THE LOADED WHEELBARROW, THE CHILD ON A BICYCLE — BUT ALSO LEAD THE EYE TOWARDS INDIVIDUAL FEATURES OF THE GARDEN LAYOUT. EVEN THE MATERIALS USED TO SURFACE THEM CAN MAKE A MAJOR CONTRIBUTION TO THE OVERALL APPEARANCE OF THE GARDEN.

Right: The path through this densely-planted garden is formed by laying square paving slabs on the diagonal and infilling along the edges with gravel to encourage ground-cover plants to encroach on it.

PLANNING A PATH

Whether the path you want is to be a major garden feature or will simply enable you to walk to the garden shed without getting your feet wet, it deserves some planning. Of course, in a very small garden your options will be severely limited, and you may have no choice but to lay it as a straight line, perhaps bordering a flower bed that hugs one boundary of your property. However, if you have more space available you can experiment with different positions and also with different layouts.

The best way of doing this is to draw up a scale plan of your garden, with all its existing features drawn in. You can then pencil in the various options; a straight path down one side or down the centre, short straights with angled corners to change the path direction, a simple curve or a meandering S-shape are all possibilities. Whatever you draw, make the path at least 1 m (just over 3 ft) wide if possible; the absolute practical minimum width is about 750 mm (2 ft 6 in).

Once you have an outline you like the look of, move outdoors with a handful of pegs or garden canes and start transferring your plan to the garden. Then go upstairs (or climb steps to eaves level if you live in a bungalow) so you can look down on the layout and check whether it works in visual terms. Ask yourself whether it is in scale with the garden. Does it leave awkward-to-mow patches of lawn alongside it?

Does it help to lead the eye towards a particularly attractive garden feature – a pond, a summerhouse, a showpiece shrub? Do not be afraid to alter the line and shape as you please; it is far simpler to move a few pegs now than to make alterations once you start to lay the path itself. Once you are happy with the layout, drive the pegs in securely in their final positions. Add stringlines to delineate straight edges, and use rope or lengths of garden hose to mark out curves, ready for the site preparation to begin.

CHOOSING MATERIALS

When you are planning a path down the garden, it is well worth thinking about the various materials available before making your final decision, since this could affect the practicality of your proposed scheme. This is particularly important if you want a path with curves, since some materials can cope better than others.

Path surfaces need to satisfy three main criteria: they should look good, wear well and be reasonably easy to keep in good condition. The materials that best satisfy these requirements are concrete, the various forms of slab and block paving, both loose-laid and mortar-bedded, gravel and tar macadam. Each has its advantages and disadvantages.

CONCRETE

Concrete is probably the most widely-used material for garden paths. It can be used as the final surface, or to provide a solid sub-base for other materials, and its main advantages are that it is extremely durable if it is mixed, laid and finished carefully, that it can easily be laid in curves and other complex shapes, and that it is fairly easy to keep in good condition. Its drawbacks revolve mainly around the laborious and time-consuming effort needed to prepare the site, mix and lay the concrete and finish the surface, and there is the added nuisance that the path cannot be used until the concrete has hardened fully.

Buying ready-mixed concrete reduces the labour element but will push up the price by as much as 30 per cent compared with mixing it yourself, and is really only worth considering if you are laying more than about 1cu m (1.3 cu yd) of concrete. You can find local

Below: Planters and beds edged with natural stone blocks complement the crazy-paved paths in this walled garden.

suppliers in your classified telephone directory under the heading Concrete – ready-mixed.

Paving

After concrete, paving of one sort or another is the second most popular material for paths. The choice includes:
• square, rectangular or hexagonal flagstones;
• small block pavers – clay or concrete blocks and paving bricks;
• crazy paving – essentially broken pieces of paving or natural stone laid in a jigsaw pattern.

All three can be laid as 'rigid' paving in a mortar bed, ideally over a concrete base if they are to last well. The first two, flagstones and pavers, can also be laid as 'flexible' paving over a bed of sand.

The advantages of paved finishes are that you have a wide choice of surface finishes and an easy-to-maintain surface.

Left: *Plain slabs are ideal for creating regular formal paths. Here, the line is broken by spacing the slabs slightly so that grass can grow between them.*

gravel in place – paths need fixed edging of some sort to stop the stones finding their way onto lawns and flower beds. One other obvious drawback is that gravel simply does not work on sloping sites.

TAR MACADAM (ASPHALT)

Tar macadam consists of crushed stone bound together with tar or asphalt and rolled out to give a flat surface. It is usually black, but red may also be available to special order, and the colour monotony can sometimes be relieved by rolling white chippings into the finished surface to give it a speckled appearance. It can be laid like concrete as a complete path, usually about 75 mm (3 in) thick, or as a surface dressing about 15 mm (⅝ in) thick over an existing sound concrete or paved surface.

Macadam needs minimal maintenance once laid, and is easy to repair if the surface is damaged. However, it is softened by prolonged hot sunshine, and can be dented by point loads. Freshly-laid macadam needs to harden for two or three days before being used.

Left: *This path features a mosaic-like pattern of small stone setts laid in diamond shapes, with the spaces filled in with gravel in a similar grey colour.*

Below: *Gravel is ideal for surfacing wide, sweeping paths, but care must be taken to keep stones from spreading onto adjoining lawns and flower beds.*

Flexible paving has the additional advantages of being relatively quick to lay, ready for immediate use and easy to repair, while rigid paving has the major drawback of involving a lot more work – especially the pointing between the slabs once they have been laid.

GRAVEL

Gravel paths have an unmistakeably 'country house' feel about them, but there is no reason why they should not be laid on a smaller scale in the average garden. For the best looks and performance, you need well-rounded pea gravel or crushed stone between 10 and 20 mm (⅜ to ¾ in) in diameter, laid about 50 mm (2 in) thick on a sub-base of hardcore which is covered with sand to stop the gravel sinking into it.

The main advantages of gravel are that it is inexpensive, that it is very quick to lay, and incidentally that it is a not inconsiderable burglar deterrent - few would-be thieves will try tip-toeing up a gravel path at dead of night. Set against that is the need for regular raking and weedkilling to keep the surface looking smart, and the problem of keeping the

PATHS

Laying a macadam path from scratch is really a job for a specialist contractor, since the macadam must be delivered, laid (in two coats) and rolled hot. Unfortunately, there are a lot of rogue macadam operatives around, who are likely to turn up on your doorstep, lay a path that will not set for months and then disappear without trace. So if you decide you want a professionally-laid path you can trust to be of good quality, only employ firms that are members of the relevant building trade associations.

If you like the look of tar macadam and want just a surface dressing over an existing path, you can use cold-roll macadam or pre-mixed asphalt. This is sold in sacks and is simply raked out and levelled with a garden roller.

PLANNING THE WORK

Once you have decided which material to use, and whether you are laying from scratch or just resurfacing an existing path or drive, you have to make your mind up as to whether you are going to do the work yourself or employ someone to do it for you. Then you must gather information on material prices for a do-it-yourself job, or get estimates from contractors, so you can budget the job properly.

For concrete, measure the length and width of the area to be covered and multiply by the thickness to be laid. So a 20 m (65 ft) long path 1 m (3 ft 3 in) wide and 100 mm (4 in) thick will need 20 x 1 x 0.1 = 2 cu m (2.6 cu yd) of concrete.

For paving slabs and blocks, divide the total path area by the individual slab or block area to get the total number of slabs/blocks needed. Add an extra 5 per cent to allow for cutting and breakages. If they will be laid on a 50 mm (2 in) thick sand bed, use the same sums as for concrete to estimate how much sand will be needed.

If you are laying gravel, take the advice of your local aggregate supplier. Lastly, a standard-sized bag of cold-roll macadam covers about 1 sq m (11 sq ft).

LAYING CONCRETE

For a garden path you need a sub-base of well-compacted hardcore covered with a top layer of sand; this is then covered with concrete laid within timber formwork. Make both the sub-base and concrete surface layer 50 mm (2 in) thick for a path taking just light foot traffic, and 75 mm (3 in) thick if it will carry heavier loads such as a wheelbarrow.

If you are mixing the concrete yourself, the mix to use is 1 part cement to 1 parts sharp sand and 2½ parts 20 mm (¾ in) aggregate; if you are using combined sand and aggregate ('all-in aggregate'), mix 1 part cement to 3½ parts aggregate. Measure out the quantities accurately by bucket rather

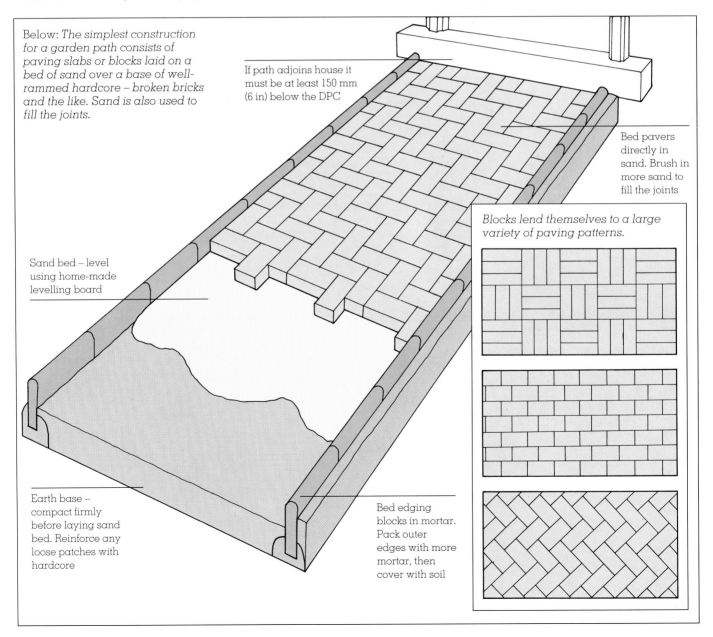

Below: *The simplest construction for a garden path consists of paving slabs or blocks laid on a bed of sand over a base of well-rammed hardcore – broken bricks and the like. Sand is also used to fill the joints.*

If path adjoins house it must be at least 150 mm (6 in) below the DPC

Bed pavers directly in sand. Brush in more sand to fill the joints

Sand bed – level using home-made levelling board

Blocks lend themselves to a large variety of paving patterns.

Earth base – compact firmly before laying sand bed. Reinforce any loose patches with hardcore

Bed edging blocks in mortar. Pack outer edges with more mortar, then cover with soil

than by shovelfuls, and hire a concrete mixer to ensure thorough, even mixing of each batch.

If you are ordering ready-mixed concrete, the specification to ask for is: minimum cement content 330 kg per cu m (20lbs per cu ft); 4 per cent entrained air; target slump 75 mm (3 in).

Excavate the path site to the required depth, set up your formwork using strong timber pegs and lay the hardcore. Then shovel the concrete into the formwork, rake it out roughly level and tamp it down with a heavy beam resting on the formwork at each side. Finish the surface with a float, a shovel back or a broom to taste. To prevent the continuous ribbon of concrete from cracking, you should then create expansion joints in the path. To do this, simply tamp a length of angle iron into the surface at roughly 2 m (6 ft) intervals and withdraw it to leave a groove about 25 mm (1 in) deep. Leave the concrete to cure under polythene sheeting or damp sacks for three days. It can then be walked on, but avoid heavy traffic for a few more days, especially in cold weather. Avoid laying concrete altogether if the ground is frozen or if frost is forecast.

LAYING FLAGSTONES AND PAVERS

You can lay both flagstones and pavers directly over an existing concrete base if this does not cause problems with levels (especially next to house walls), so long as the old concrete is in good condition. If it is not, it is best to break it up and use it as hardcore for a new sub-base. If you are laying a sub-base from scratch, it should be 75 mm (3 in) thick for a path taking light foot traffic, and 100 mm (4 in) or more for paths carrying heavier loads.

If you plan to bed the flagstones, crazy paving or brick pavers in mortar, use a 1:5 cement:sand mix. Place the mortar in a 'box-and-cross' pattern beneath large slabs – a line round the perimeter of the slab and crossed lines in the centre – and tamp the slab down into position. With crazy paving and small brick or block pavers, use a continuous mortar bed. When all the slabs or blocks are laid, point the joints, using a dry crumbly mortar mix so you do not stain the face of the stones. You will have to use a small pointing trowel on crazy paving, but for flagstones and pavers with narrow regular-sized joints it is easier to use a strip of plywood or hardboard to ram the mortar into the joints, finishing it about 3 mm (⅛ in) below the surface of the paving.

If you are laying flagstones or flexible paving on a sand bed, you need a thicker sub-base – about 100 mm (4 in) of well-compacted hardcore on sandy soil, more on clay soil. Follow the advice of

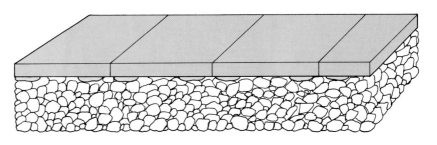
Pre-cast slabs resting on five mortar spots over compacted hardcore

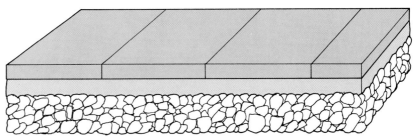
Pre-cast slabs laid on a layer of mortar over compacted hardcore

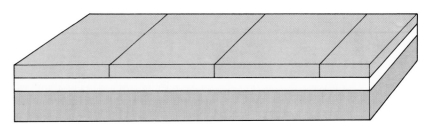
Pre-cast slabs laid on a bed of sand over compacted soil

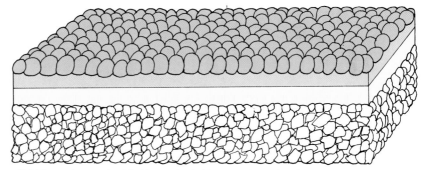
Cobble paving, embedded in mortar laid on sand over hardcore

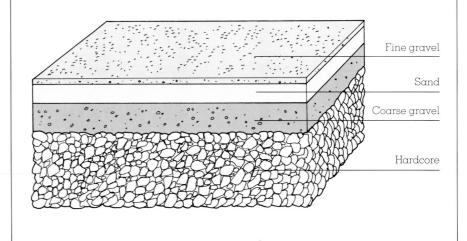
Fine gravel

Sand

Coarse gravel

Hardcore

the block manufacturers on this point. You also need some form of edge restraints – pegged timber, kerbstones or blocks set on edge in concrete – to stop the slabs or blocks from creeping outwards at the edges and to prevent the sand bed from eroding. You then top the sub-base with a 50 mm (2 in) thick layer of sharp sand, and place the slabs or blocks in position. Once they have all been bedded into place and tamped down, brush more sand over the surface to fill the joints, but remember that since the paving is laid on a flexible bed of sand they may tend to open up and crack the pointing as time goes by.

LAYING GRAVEL

This is the simplest way of laying a new path. All you need is enough 10-20 mm (⅜ – ¾ in) diameter pea gravel to form a layer about 50 mm (2 in) thick over the path area; your supplier will advise you on how much to order. You will find local suppliers listed in your classified telephone directory under Quarries or Sand and gravel suppliers, or you can ask at your local builders' merchants.

To lay a gravel path, simply excavate the area to a depth of about 150 mm (6 in) – or 200 mm (8 in) on soft clay soils – and ram in a 100 to 150 mm (4 to 6 in) thick layer of hardcore. Add some coarse gravel and then a layer of sand to prevent the gravel from sinking into the sub-base. Then install some form of

perimeter edging – pegged strips of preservative-treated timber, for example, or path edging stones or brick pavers set in concrete. Once they are in place, you can have the gravel delivered. You will probably need to barrow it to the path site, so set planks on the lawn if you have to run across it. Simply shovel it in between the edge restraints, spread it out, rake it level, and the path is ready for use.

It is a good idea to keep a couple of sacks of gravel over from the job, so you can fill ruts and top up bald patches as the path wears and settles down. It will need raking regularly, plus treatment with weedkiller two or three times a year.

LAYING COLD-ROLL MACADAM (COLD-MIX ASPHALT)

As mentioned earlier, laying hot macadam is really a job best left to professional contractors. However, you can lay cold-roll macadam over old concrete, paving or existing macadam to give it a new surface if it is sound but looks in need of a facelift. It is difficult to lay this product over hardcore with an ordinary garden roller – you need to put down two layers and use a hired plate vibrator to get good results – and so it is best not used to create new paths from scratch.

The material comes in sacks, generally containing 25 kg (55 lb) which will cover an area of about 1sq m (11sq ft) in

a layer 20 mm (¾ in) thick as raked out and 15 mm (⅝ in) thick after rolling and compacting. You will also need a quantity of liquid bitumen emulsion for use as a tack coat over the existing surface. A 5 kg (11 lb) drum will cover an area of about 7 sq m (75 sq ft).

Start by preparing the old path surface, filling potholes with macadam after brushing in some bitumen emulsion to improve the adhesion of the repair. Then pour the bitumen emulsion onto the surface, brush it out with an old broom and leave it to become tacky – this takes a couple of hours. Throw the broom head away afterwards.

Next, tip out the bags and rake the macadam out to a thickness of about 20 mm (¾ in). It is best to work in imaginary bays about 1 m (3 ft) wide. Use the back of the rake to break down any lumps, and check the surface as you work for slopes, bumps and hollows using a spirit level and a timber straight-edge. When you have got it reasonably level, roll the surface with a garden roller, filling in any hollows that appear using some extra macadam. Keep the roller wet by sprinkling water onto it from a watering can so it does not pick up lumps of macadam. Finish off by scattering contrasting stone chippings over the surface and rolling them in.

You can walk on the path surface immediately, but avoid heavy traffic for two or three days to allow the binder to harden fully.

STEPS

IF YOU HAVE A GARDEN THAT SLOPES STEEPLY OR IS ALREADY ON SEVERAL DIFFERENT LEVELS, STEPS ARE THE OBVIOUS WAY OF COPING WITH THE SLOPE OR OF GETTING FROM ONE LEVEL TO THE NEXT. APART FROM THEIR PRACTICAL VALUE, THEY CAN ALSO BE A PLEASING GARDEN FEATURE IN THEIR OWN RIGHT. YOU CAN USE THEM EITHER TO LINK SEPARATE FLAT AREAS OF THE GARDEN, SUCH AS LAWNS AND TERRACES, OR TO MAKE PATHS UP STEEP SLOPES EASIER TO NEGOTIATE.

You can build steps as free-standing structures, usually where a wall separates the higher and lower areas, or cut them into the slope of the land itself. You can, of course, also have 'cut-in' steps where a wall occurs, by cutting back into the upper level so that the bottom step is flush with the face of the wall instead of being some distance away from it. Cut-in steps are generally easier to build, because the ground provides most of the support for the treads and very little complicated masonry is involved, but you do not have to be highly skilled to create perfectly satisfactory free-standing steps if that is the type you prefer.

The easiest ways of building garden steps are either to use garden walling blocks and paving slabs, or to cast them in concrete. The former method is far simpler than the latter, which tends to look aesthetically ugly anyway. The two

Above: If you leave narrow planting pockets at the rear of each tread on a flight of natural stone steps, low-level plants will soften their appearance.

most important factors to remember are that the materials you choose should suit the style of your garden – in other words, they should blend in with walls, paved areas and other masonry features – and that they should be safe to use.

PRELIMINARY PLANNING

Start by deciding what materials you are going to use, since this could affect the dimensions of the steps. For example, risers in blockwork should ideally be two blocks (about 150 mm/6 in) high. The size of the paving slabs you choose will dictate the tread width (and perhaps its depth, although cut slabs at

the rear of the tread are perfectly acceptable). Remember that for safety, treads should measure at least 300 mm (12 in) from front to rear, so that your toe or heel does not catch the edge of the step above as you ascend or descend the flight. Furthermore, the flight should have a minimum width of 600 mm (2 ft), and 1200 mm (4 ft) or more if people will want to pass each other on the flight.

The next stage is to work out how many steps the flight needs, by measuring the vertical height between the two levels and dividing this by the height of an individual riser. Remember that the bottom step height will include the tread thickness, but the others will not. If the answer you get from this piece of arithmetic is not close to a whole number, vary the riser height; for comfortable (and safe) walking combine shallower risers with deeper treads, higher risers with shallower treads. Do not build risers higher than about 170 mm (7 in); they are tiring to climb on all but very short flights, and can be a trip hazard.

Now you can make some simple sketches showing the plan and the front and side elevations of the flight, so you can work out the bonding pattern for the masonry and therefore estimate how many blocks and pavers you will need for the job.

As you make your plans, remember that free-standing steps should be toothed into the wall from which they are built out, to prevent them from pulling away from it if the flight should subside slightly. Cut-in types are not so prone to movement, but on steep slopes it is a good idea to set the lowest riser on a concrete strip foundation for extra stability. Where a flight will exceed about seven steps, you should include a landing – a wider flat area – at the halfway point.

Do not forget to provide drainage so water does not collect on the treads; this will make them slippery and potentially dangerous, and will also encourage the growth of algae and moss on their surfaces. Standing water will also freeze in winter – an obvious but oft-forgotten hazard, as any hospital casualty department will confirm. You should allow a fall of about 12 mm (½ in) towards the front of each tread.

Think too about drainage from paved areas at the bottom of the flight; in wet weather the steps can act as a small waterfall and may carry water from an upper area down to the lower one in unexpectedly large quantities. A gully leading to a nearby soakaway may be the answer.

STEPS

It is essential to fit a handrail or build parapet walls beside long flights, especially if they will be used by children or the elderly. Ensure that tread nosings project beyond the face of each riser, to throw a shadow and accentuate the edge of the tread. Provide lighting if the steps will be used at night.

SITE PREPARATION

Once you have completed the planning and taken delivery of the materials you ordered, you can start to mark out and excavate the site of your steps. How you proceed depends on the type of steps you are building.

For free-standing steps you need a concrete strip foundation beneath the perimeter of the lowest flight. This should be 100 mm (4 in) thick and 230 mm (9 in) wide for stretcher-bond blockwork. For flights more than five treads high, the individual risers need to be supported too, so rather than laying individual strip foundations for them it is better to lay a concrete foundation slab big enough to support the whole flight. For both strip and slab foundations, allow the concrete to set hard before building on it – 24–48 hours is usually enough, but in cold climates allow three days in summer and up to six in winter. Cover it with polythene or damp sacking to stop it from drying too quickly in hot weather.

For cut-in steps, the slope itself is cut away into steps to support the individual treads. Use string lines to mark the width of the flight and the position of the nosing of each tread. Then dig out the rough shape of each step in turn, working from the bottom of the flight upwards. Check as you work that each step is approximately the same depth and height, and take care not to break down the leading edges of the steps as you work. To lessen the risk of step edges crumbling as you excavate them, stand on a short board or plywood offcut slightly smaller than the tread itself to spread your weight.

Use a tamping post to pack down any small patches of loose subsoil you come across. If you find larger 'soft spots', dig them out until you reach firm subsoil, and pack in hardcore to restore the level.

For long or steep flights, cast a concrete strip foundation across the line of the lowest riser for extra support. It should be 100 mm (4 in) thick and twice as wide as the riser thickness.

THE FIRST STEP

Once you have completed the site preparation and laid the foundations, you are ready to start building your steps. Check first that you have all the necessary tools and materials to hand.

For laying garden walling blocks, use a 1:5 mortar mix with added plasticiser, or else buy bagged dry ready-mixed bricklaying mortar – a 50 kg (112 lb) bag makes enough mortar to lay about 60 bricks. If you are mixing your own mortar, one 50 kg bag of cement plus soft bricklaying sand will yield enough mortar for at least 450 bricks.

For free-standing steps, start by setting out pairs of string lines over the centre of your strip foundations to mark the outline of the first course of blocks (1). Then lay mortar along the front of the foundations and bed the first course of the riser in it. Check that the front edge of the riser is the correct distance from the wall; then complete the first course, working back towards the wall at each side and cutting the last block to size if necessary.

Use your builder's square to check the corners for accuracy, and adjust them if they are out of square.

You can now add the second course (2), in whatever bonding pattern you have decided to adopt. Where the course meets the wall, chop out a wall block and tooth in the last whole block of the step course (3, p50).

Allow the mortar to harden, then shovel in hardcore behind the riser and tamp it down. Take care not to disturb the new work as you do this.

On long flights of steps, you should build up walls off the foundation slab beneath the positions of subsequent risers to provide support for the treads (4, p50). Then add hardcore as before.

Right: *This unusual flight of steps zig-zags its way up the bank, with the individual treads supported on separate cast concrete blocks. The risers are kept low for safety reasons.*

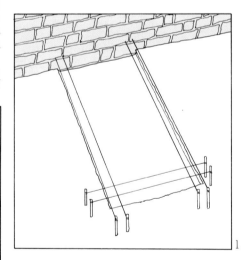

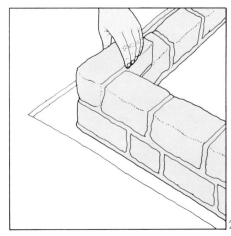

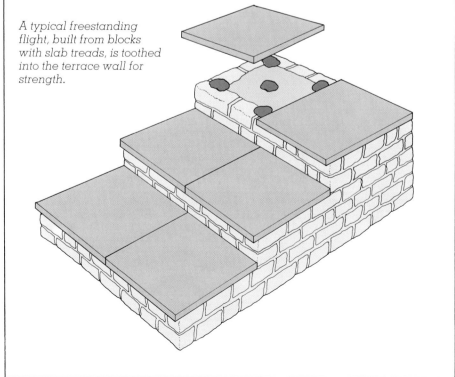

A typical freestanding flight, built from blocks with slab treads, is toothed into the terrace wall for strength.

If the steps are to be flanked by parapet walls, you are likely to be working in 230 mm (9 in) thick blockwork. Here the treads will rest on the inner half of the wall, with the outer 'skin' continuing unbroken past each tread position. With risers two blocks high, it is best to use English bond – alternate courses of stretchers and headers – with the stretcher course being used alongside each tread position so that the treads rest on the inner half of the headers on every other course.

With cut-in steps, all you have to do is to spread a bed of mortar over the compacted subsoil (or on the strip foundation if one is being used) and build up the riser in stretcher bond, cutting blocks as necessary to match the tread width. Then back-fill behind the riser with subsoil if there is a gap, tamping it down to just below the level of the top of the riser.

With free-standing steps the treads are added when the flight is completed (see COMPLETING THE FLIGHTS opposite), but with cut-in steps the second riser is usually built off the back edge of the first tread. Bed the slabs that form the tread in position, with a continuous mortar bed on top of the riser and generous dabs of mortar on the hardcore. Tamp the slabs down, check that they are level from side to side and ensure that there is a slight fall from back to front. Remember that for safety the front edge of the tread – the nosing – should project beyond the face of the riser below by a distance of about 25 mm (1 in).

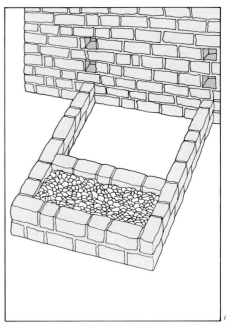

THE SECOND STEP

Building the second step of your flight is just a repeat of the previous stage, except that for free-standing steps the U-shaped retaining wall is shallower from front to back.

For free-standing steps, you once again build the riser first - off the hardcore packing on short flights, on top of the honeycomb supporting wall you built within the previous flight on long ones. Check that the riser's front edge is

the correct distance from the wall behind, then complete the blockwork according to your plans. Again, tooth in the second course of the riser to the wall, and back-fill with hardcore (5). Continue raising honeycomb supporting walls to support the remaining risers further up the flight as necessary.

For cut-in steps, you simply bed the blocks to form the second riser on the rear edge of the first tread, then back-fill behind it and bed the second tread in place. Again, check that the tread is level from side to side and that it slopes

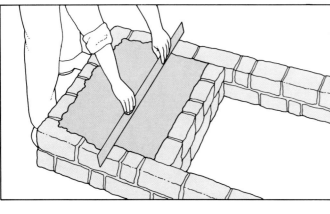

slightly from front to back. Spread your weight as you work on the second tread by laying a board on top of the first one.

COMPLETING THE FLIGHTS

Continue this sequence of operations to build the rest of the flight, adding risers (and treads on cut-in steps) until you reach the top (6).

With free-standing steps, the last riser you build will usually finish one step below the upper level; the wall itself will form the last riser, and the top tread will be level with (or will be part of) the upper level.

When you have finished all the brick-laying and the backfilling is consolidated, you can lay the treads. Start with the bottom step, laying a generous dabs of mortar on top of the supporting block-work and adding dabs of mortar on top

of the hardcore (7). Then set each tread in position, tamping it down as described for cut-in steps and checking the level and the drainage slope (8). Point the gap between the rear edge of the tread and the next riser neatly, or add cut pavers at the rear of deep treads. Then add subsequent treads in the same way, and finish off by neatening off all the pointing. As before, use a board to spread your weight when standing on treads you have just laid to avoid disturbing them.

If the flight is flanked by parapet walls, continue to build these up to the required height. Cut blocks at an angle as necessary if the line of the wall is to match the slope of the flight, and finish off the wall with pre-cast coping stones or a soldier course of blocks set on edge and neatly pointed. If you are adding a soldier course of blocks, use small

galvanised ties to secure the end block in place; it is prone to being dislodged accidentally otherwise.

With cut-in steps, all that remains is to neaten the pointing on the risers and between the treads, and to fill in the edges of the flight with turf or soil as appropriate.

Try to avoid using your new steps for at least 48 hours after you have finished building them, to allow the mortar to set hard. Set up simple rope barricades to remind the forgetful.

CONCRETE STEPS

As already mentioned, steps built with block risers and slab treads are probably the most popular form of garden step construction, but cast concrete steps are an alternative. However, setting up the timber formwork is quite complicated and the finish is utilitarian, to say the least, unless it is faced with some other material. However, concrete steps are very durable and may be worth considering as part of a patio or path project involving the use of lots of concrete for the other surfaces.

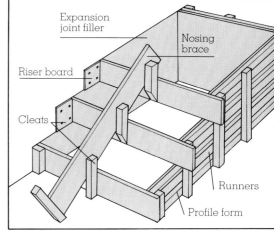

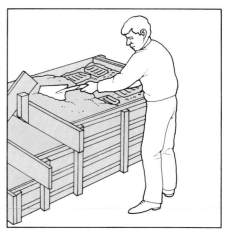

Left: *Concrete steps are an economical alternative to masonry, especially for longer flights. A coat of masonry paint can give them a brighter look.*

STEPS

If you are casting concrete steps in a bank, excavate the slope as for cut-in paved steps. Then cast a 150 mm (6 in) thick concrete foundation strip beneath the position of the first step. Position the formwork so that the front of each tread will overlap the back of the one below it by about 150 mm (6 in), so that each tread is bonded to its neighbours. Remember to give the formwork at the sides of each tread a slight slope towards the front. Start placing the concrete at the foot of the flight, laying each succeeding step in turn. Tamp the concrete down level with the tops of the formwork, and leave this in place for at least 48 hours before removing it. Give the steps a further two or three days to harden fully before using them.

To cast free-standing concrete steps the formwork must be much stronger and the whole flight must be built on a 150 mm (6 in) thick concrete foundation. The practical maximum height for a flight of this sort is about five treads.

Use 12 mm (½ in) plywood cut to the shape of the flight for the sides, bracing them upright with braces and stakes, and nail on the formers for the tread fronts. Start filling the formwork with concrete, then top this with a layer of steel reinforcing mesh. When the rest of the concrete has been poured in, it will set round the mesh and help to bond the flight together. Again, leave the concrete to harden – this time for four or five days because of the mass of concrete involved – before carefully removing the formwork.

In areas where winter frost is very cold and prolonged, foundations may need to be considerably deeper than the measurements given above to ensure that they are below the frost line. Consult local building codes for guidance, or take professional advice.

Right: *Steps are the natural way to link different levels of sloping gardens.*

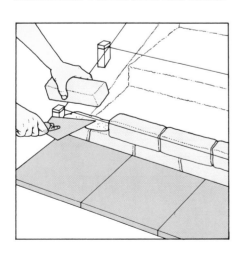

1 Mark out the flight with pegs and stringlines, and excavate the step shapes. Then lay the lowest slabs and fill in behind them with hardcore and mortar.

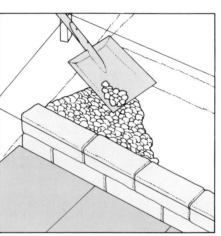

3 Fill in behind the first riser with hardcore, and check that the step cut in the bank is roughly level with the top of the masonry. Dig deeper if necessary.

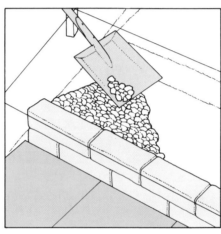

2 Build up the brickwork or blockwork to form the first riser, checking that the masonry is level and neatening the pointing as you complete each course.

4 Tamp a little hardcore into the step to consolidate the soil, and to provide a slight fall from the back to the front of the step cut-out for drainage.

5 Back-fill the next step with more hardcore and tamp down as before. Then lay the slabs to form the second tread, again with a slight overhang at the front.

Below: Even a shallow flight of built-in steps makes an attractive garden feature.

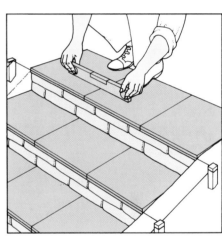

8 Carry on building risers and laying treads until you reach the top of the flight, setting the last tread level with the ground at the top of the bank.

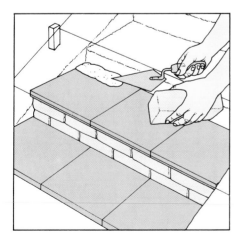

6 Lay the next course of bricks or blocks to form the second riser on the back edge of the first tread. Keep mortar off the rest of the slab to avoid staining.

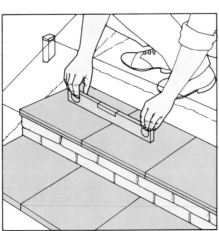

7 Place pats of mortar on the hardcore, plus more on the first riser, and lay the slabs that will form the next tread. Check that they are level across the tread.

9 Neaten the pointing on the risers and brush a dry sand/mortar mix into the joints between the slabs. Leave for about seven days to set before using them.

53

PLANTERS

Apart from having masonry features on a grand scale, such as walls, patios, paths and steps, every garden needs smaller details too to provide some variation in scale. Planters are a perfect example, and by working with suitable raw materials you will soon be able to create a whole range of different-sized and shaped plant containers that will enhance the corner of the patio or sit tantalisingly at the edge of a flower bed or shrubbery. So long as their soil is watered regularly, whatever you choose to grow in your planters will thrive and help to produce an attractive garden ornament.

If you are going to carve stone, as opposed to just cutting it, you will need some special mason's tools and a club hammer to drive them. The basic cutting and shaping tool is a chisel, an all-steel construction with a hexagonal cross-section and a square-ended cutting blade; it is available in sizes ranging from 12 to 50 mm (½ to 2 in) wide. The point chisel or punch, as its name implies, has a pointed cutting tip, and is used to concentrate the force of the hammer on a small area of the stone during the initial roughing-out of the workpiece. The pitching tool has a wide single-ground blade, and is used for removing larger amounts of stone when trimming a workpiece down to the required size.

For carving the sort of cut-out necessary to create a stone planter, the most versatile tool of all is a mason's scutch holder, a special chisel-like tool with a replaceable cutting edge known as a scutch. This is double-sided, and may have plain or toothed edges. It is used after the initial roughing-out, and the toothed version leaves a series of furrows in the stone which can either be left as

Right: *Simple carved planters blend well with the garden, and are an ideal introduction to stone-carving techniques.*

Below: *You need only the simplest carving tools to create both formal and irregularly-shaped planters.*

the final finish or can be smoothed off using either the plain mason's chisel or the wider mason's bolster.

CHOOSING STONE

The best types of stone to use for carving objects such as garden planters are the various sandstones and limestones. Both can be liable to frost damage in the long term if they are used in a permanently damp situation, while limestone will be gradually eroded by rainwater action. However, the latter will do minimal damage over the likely life of the planter, and will have the beneficial effect of rendering it self-cleansing.

In order to minimise the amount of cutting and wastage involved in carving the planter, try to choose stones that are already rough-cut to about the size and

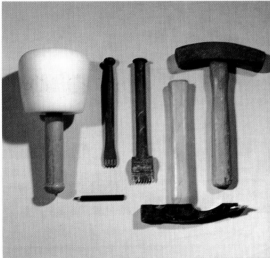

Above: *Basic carving tools include hammers, mallets, mason's chisels, and a scutch holder and scutch.*

overall depth you want. As far as colour is concerned, both types of stone can be found in shades ranging from creamy white to deep ochre; limestones may contain visible shell and other fossil formations, betraying their submarine origins, while the sandstones may have bands of colour resulting from the depositing of different-coloured sediments during their formation. These can look particularly attractive as an edge detail to small pieces of ornamental stonework such as a garden planter.

When selecting stones, remember that even small pieces can be surprisingly heavy – the typical density of limestones and sandstones is between 2,000 and 2,500 kilograms per cubic metre (125 to 155 pounds per cubic foot). Turn stones on the ground to inspect them, with the help of a sturdy lever and fulcrum if necessary to get extra power, and do not lift heavy stones without

Planters

help. When it comes to transporting them, take great care not to overload and damage the suspension of the typical family car, which was not designed to carry such loads.

See pages 86-87 for more details about selecting stone.

Carving a planter

When you have found a suitable piece of stone in an appropriate size, shape and colour for your garden, examine it carefully to see which way the 'bed' of the stone runs (see below). Although limestone and sandstone are both relatively soft, you will find carving much easier if you are working with the bed horizontal, cutting into it and then hollowing out along it rather than the other way round.

Before starting to mark out and carve the stone, set it at a comfortable height on a sturdy support; a tailor-made timber carving table 600 to 750 mm (24 to 30 in) square is ideal.

1 Start by marking the outline of the recess you want to cut in pencil on the top surface of the stone. Leave a margin between the cutting line and the edge of the stone of at least 50 mm (2 in), to avoid any risk of the edge breaking away as you work.
2 Use a club hammer and mason's chisel – or better still a toothed scutch in a mason's scutch holder – to outline the recess. Work all round the cutting line, chopping vertically downwards first, then lower the tool's cutting angle to about 45° to start breaking away the

stone within it. Always work towards the centre of the recess, walking round the workpiece as you do so.
3 As the recess deepens, brush out the stone chippings and dust so you can keep a close eye on your progress.
4 Continue carving in the same way, gradually deepening the recess by cutting down the sides further to create a smooth bowl in the stone. Check the depth of the recess as you work, to avoid any risk of cutting too deep and cracking the stone or breaking through the base.
5 Either leave the stone with the ridged finish left by the toothed scutch, or smooth off the ridges using a plain scutch, a mason's chisel or a bolster. Brush out the debris for the last time and the planter is ready for use.

4

5

MAKING A WORK TABLE

Use workshop scrap wood and a blockboard offcut to assemble a sturdy carving work table with a comfortable working height. Cut the pieces to length and nail them securely together.

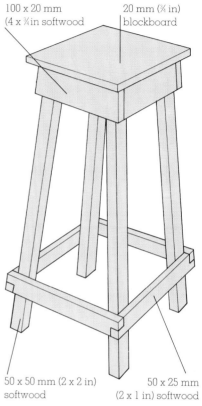

100 x 20 mm
(4 x ⅜ in softwood

20 mm (¾ in)
blockboard

50 x 50 mm (2 x 2 in)
softwood

50 x 25 mm
(2 x 1 in) softwood

Left: *Working at ground level is always possible, but it can cause back-ache, so a custom-made table (Above) is best.*

ROCKERIES

CREATING A ROCKERY OR ROCK GARDEN NOT ONLY ADDS A WELCOME THIRD DIMENSION TO THE EXPANSE OF LAWNS AND FLOWERBEDS FOUND IN A TYPICAL GARDEN. IT ALSO BRINGS A VARIETY OF TEXTURE TO THE GARDEN AND ALLOWS YOU TO GROW A VARIETY OF SPECIES SUCH AS ALPINE PLANTS WHICH WILL MAKE THE ROCKERY A COLOURFUL AND INTERESTING GARDEN FEATURE ALL THE YEAR ROUND.

In their natural habitat, rock plants grow and thrive in the wind-blown soil and broken-down stone chippings that always accumulate in pockets in the rocks and around the base of the outcrop. The contrast between the mass of stone and the delicacy of the tiny plants makes a striking contrast, and is one that gardeners everywhere have long striven to emulate on a smaller scale in their own gardens.

The secret of success in creating a rock garden is not to try to emulate the sometimes strikingly massive rockeries on view in large parks and botanical gardens. There is still space for a rock garden in even a small plot, but it must be in scale with its surroundings.

CHOOSING A SITE

A successful rock garden should look just like a natural outcrop of rock, so it will work best if surrounded by an expanse of lawn or other open space. It should be kept well away from formal features such as regular flower beds, paths and geometrically-shaped ponds, since its own informality will sit uneasily alongside them. However, including a rock pool in a rock garden, perhaps with a cascade or waterfall, can look most attractive.

If you are too short of space to site your rock garden in the open, you can build it up against a garden wall or in a corner between two walls, although this

Right: On sloping sites, use the largest blocks you can find to create a rockery in scale with the bank. Make sure the stones are securely bedded.

Below: On level sites, keep the rockery structure relatively low; tall mounds look out of place, and nature would have quickly eroded a high outcrop of rock.

never quite looks as natural as it should. Never build one against a house wall, where it can cause damp penetration.

If the garden slopes, this gives you the opportunity to use the slope to good effect, letting the rocks break through the natural ground level, and if the slope is steep you can build the rocks up as a natural outcrop that in practice also acts as an earth-retaining wall if the stones are big enough.

Choose a site which gets plenty of sunshine, since most alpine plants prefer full sun to shade (where, in their natural habitat, they would freeze to

for the rock gardener, but are likely to prove comparatively expensive.

When choosing stones, look mainly for flattish slabs rather than rounded boulders, and pick pieces in a range of sizes which will help to give the rockery a natural appearance. Do not attempt to take them home by car, even in several separate trips; you risk damaging its suspension. If the supplier's delivery charges seem excessive, it may be worth hiring a truck and collecting the stones yourself. Take one or more strong helpers with you to assist in lifting the heavier stones.

You will also need soil for your rockery, and unless you are planning any major landscaping work in your garden and will have soil to spare, you will have to order this from your garden centre or other supplier. The ideal material is good-quality topsoil mixed with coarse sand to improve drainage.

PLANNING THE ROCKERY

The shape of rockery you build will depend to a certain extent on the size of the available site. As a general rule, avoid pure geometric shapes such as circles, rectangles or ovals; nature is never that symmetrical. Instead aim for something more random such as a tapering wedge shape, wider at the front and narrowing down as the stones rise towards the rear, which at least gives the impression that they were exposed naturally by the effects of wind and rain.

The ideal rock garden is built up in tiers, each smaller than the one beneath it. Apart from mimicking nature, this ensures that the structure is stable and will not suffer from any unexpected avalanches. On a flat site, try to ensure that the tiers look different when viewed from different angles; they should not look like the symmetrical layers of a wedding cake. On a sloping site, set each succeeding tier back into the face of the slope to create a basically triangular layout.

Do not make the mistake of building the rockery too high. To keep things in proportion, the overall height should never be more than half the diameter of the base.

PREPARING FOUNDATIONS

A rockery is more than just a random pile of stones and soil, built up on your chosen site. It needs a suitable foundation and, more importantly, good drainage, especially on a flat site or where the soil is clay rather than sand or chalk. Clay soils tend not to drain freely, and this can mean that your rockery becomes a sticky waterlogged mess after heavy rain.

Start by marking out the approximate shape you want the rockery to have. Do

death). Some will tolerate light shade, however, and you can place these on the least sunny side of the rock garden. Keep it well away from overhanging trees. Not only will they shade the rockery; if they are deciduous their annual leaf fall will be difficult to clear from the rockery and an accumulation of dead leaves will smother the plants. Watch out too for large shrubs nearby with greedy root systems, since they will rob the rock garden of moisture in hot weather.

Last of all, site your rock garden where it can be seen and enjoyed – in the front garden, or at the back in full view of the living-room window.

CHOOSING STONE

Since transport charges make up most of the cost of natural stone, it makes sense to shop for it locally. If you have any quarries nearby, they will be your best (and cheapest) sources, and will offer stone that is in keeping with the local geology. Otherwise garden centres or builders' merchants are likely to be your only source; some now stock quantities of stone in several varieties specifically

ROCKERIES

not bother with pegs and stringlines; trickling sand out round the perimeter of the area will be perfectly adequate.

Next remove any turf or vegetation from the site, and excavate it to a depth of about 150 mm (6 in). Set topsoil aside in a heap unless it is heavy clay, in which case remove it to another part of the garden. Then trample the subsoil firmly to consolidate it and create a solid base for the rockery.

The solution to poor-draining clay soils is to create a drainage sump or soakaway beneath the rockery. The natural backward tilt of the stones will tend to channel water down into the centre of the rockery, so dig out a hole there about 900 mm (3 ft) square and

450 mm (18 in) deep. Fill this with hard-core and then cover it with a layer of coarse gravel or some upturned turf to prevent topsoil from washing down into the soakaway and clogging it up.

Next, prepare the bedding material – a mixture of five parts topsoil to one part sand. The quickest way of doing this is by the shovelful, mixing five of one and one of the other in a wheelbarrow and then dumping it straight into the hole. Carry on mixing and tipping until the bedding reaches ground level (1).

BUILDING UP THE ROCKERY

Start by selecting the largest stone from your stack (2) to form the keystone of the rockery. It will be too heavy to lift unless you have help, so use a baulk of stout timber and a fulcrum to lever it end over end from the stack to the site. You may be tempted to use a pickaxe to do this; however, it was not designed to withstand leverage between head and handle, and using it in this way will weaken the fixing and may well break the handle completely.

Once the stone is in its approximate final position, look at it from every angle to check its orientation, and to make

sure that any visible strata are roughly horizontal. One face may be more presentable than another, and now is the time to swing it round to get the best face forward. As you adjust the stone's position, swivel it from side to side to settle it into the bedding material. Then insert your lever under the front edge and raise it slightly so you can shovel some more soil underneath its front edge and thereby give it a slight backward tilt. This mimics the way natural rock outcrops lie, creates natural planting pockets above each stone and also helps to guide rainwater back into the rockery instead of making it cascade down over the stones and wash the soil away. Compact the soil round the base of the stone thoroughly using a baulk of timber, then stand on it to check that it is securely bedded with no tendency to rock from side to side.

Select two slightly smaller stones next and lay them in the same way either side of the keystone. Set them back slightly to give the front tier of the rockery its desired shape, and butt them tightly up against the keystone. Wedge small pieces of stone into any gaps to help retain soil behind the stones. Again tilt each stone backwards slightly,

each stone will safely bear your weight as proof that it is well bedded.

At this stage, stand back and review your progress. Now is the time to make any alterations to the appearance of the stones, before you start building the second tier behind them, so look carefully at the way each stone lies. Does it look as if its front face is emerging naturally from the soil beneath as if by erosion? Are its strata running at a natural-looking angle? Are the stones closely butted together so the joints look like natural fissures? Make any necessary adjustments, then shovel in more of the bedding mix behind the stones ready for the second tier to be built (3).

Stamp this bedding mixture down well to form a solid base for the next tier before starting to place the stones. Again use large stones near the centre of the tier and smaller ones at the edges (4). Experiment by setting some of the stones slightly in front of their neighbours to give the tier a jagged and more natural appearance and to vary the sizes of the planting pockets. Again set the stones with a slight backward tilt, wedge small pieces of stone between the larger ones to help retain the topsoil, and check their stability by standing on them. Rebed any that move, and make

packing soil under its front edge, and consolidate it in position.

Lay the rest of the stones in the first tier of the rockery in the same way, tapering them down in size as you work outwards towards the ends of the tier. Check that

sure that you are happy with the way the individual stones are arranged.

Add more soil behind the tier to build up the height gradually, and create as many further tiers as the design of your rockery requires,

ROCKERIES

completing the structure by placing one or two stones at the pinnacle.

The next stage is to add the growing medium – three parts of good topsoil, two parts of compost or peat and one part of coarse sand. Add some bone-meal, mix it thoroughly and spread the mixture over all the exposed soil surfaces of the rockery to a depth of about 75 mm (3 in). Firm it into place ready for planting to begin (5, p61).

Below: *If you are fortunate enough to have running water in your garden, create a series of natural rock falls and let it cascade over them.*

Once you have planted the rockery, water it well using a fine spray setting on your garden hose or sprinkler. Check whether water is running visibly through any gaps between the stones, and block them with small stone wedges. Then spread a 25 mm (1 in) thick layer of coarse stone chippings over all exposed soil surfaces. This keeps weeds down and prevents the soil from drying out in summer.

ROCKERY MAINTENANCE

A well-built rockery (6, p61) will not move significantly, although some of the stones may settle slightly as the back-fill is compacted by rain. If individual stones do show signs of movement, lift them slightly with a lever and pack smaller pieces of stone beneath them. Add fresh chippings as necessary to cover any soil that becomes exposed through natural erosion or after a cloudburst.

VARIATIONS ON A THEME

You can extend the rockery principle in many ways. For example, if you have an open boundary at the front of your property, laid at present to lawn, a linear rockery along the boundary will not only look most attractive; it will define the border clearly, and help to

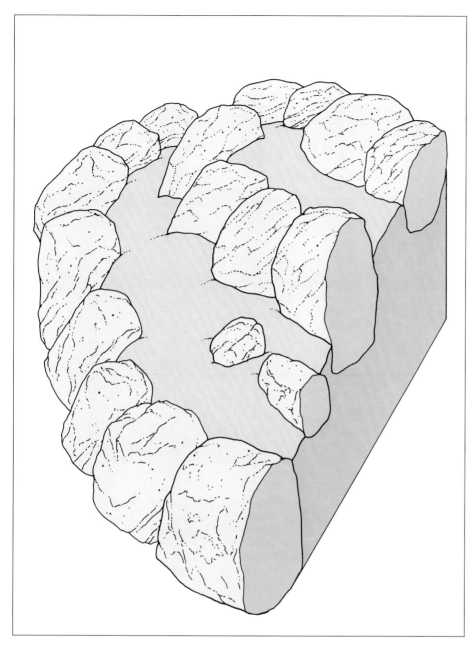

dissuade passing children or dogs from trespassing on it. Such a boundary rockery need be no more than about 1m (about 3 ft) deep and perhaps 500 mm (20 in) high, and the plants it can support will make a most unusual display all year round.

If you have a steeply sloping back garden, a vertical rockery incorporating a cascade could be a stunning centrepiece. The basic construction involves creating a closed loop for the water to run round with the aid of a pump, discharging at the top of the cascade and flowing down over the stones to a collecting pool at the foot of the slope. To keep the water from seeping away into the subsoil, this loop must obviously be waterproofed, and the best way of doing this is to use flexible pond lining material (see pages 74-76 for more details) to create a watercourse from the top of the slope down to the pool at the bottom. The pump can be submerged in this pool, and the hose is run beneath the liner up to its discharge point.

A cascade of this sort works best using fairly large stones, which must be set in steps cut in the slope to keep them in position. Work from the bottom upwards, excavating the collecting pool first; this should be as wide as the cascade but can be fairly shallow from front to back so it can be almost concealed by overhanging stones; it should also be deep enough to conceal the pump and to provide a reasonable reservoir of water for the cascade. Then cut out the steps and lay the liner in position over them, funnelling its bottom end over the lip of the collecting pool.

Spread some rounded gravel on each step to provide a bedding for the stones (and to prevent them from puncturing the liner if they have any sharp projections). Then set the stones in place, building them up so they touch each other in the random arrangement of a natural rock outcrop and so conceal the liner beneath. Set each stone so its top surface slopes downwards towards the front.

At the top, lay a flattish stone with a slight forward tilt to act as the top discharge lip of the cascade. Bring the circulating hose from behind it to near its front edge, then conceal it with a final capping stone bedded in gravel on top of the stone forming the discharge lip. Complete the cascade by wedging smaller stones into any gaps.

Now you can fill the reservoir and start the pump. Water will flow over the discharge lip and will tinkle down over and between the other stones, eventually being funnelled by the liner into the collecting pool for recirculation.

Left: *A combined rockery and pool lets you grow aquatic plants alongside your favourite rockery alpines.*

SEATS & TABLES

WHILE STONE MIGHT NOT APPEAR TO BE AN OBVIOUS CHOICE AS A MATERIAL FOR CREATING GARDEN FURNITURE, THERE IS TREMENDOUS SCOPE FOR USING ITS STRENGTH, DURABILITY AND RUGGED NATURAL APPEARANCE TO CREATE SEATS AND TABLES THAT CAN REMAIN AS A PERMANENT PART OF THE LANDSCAPE EVEN WHEN THEY ARE NOT BEING USED FOR THEIR PRIMARY PURPOSE.

BUILDING STONE SEATS

For anyone who has ever walked in the countryside and has looked for a natural seat to rest on from time to time, it takes relatively little imagination to transplant that welcome shelf of stone on the open hillside into the garden. The stone bench – perhaps a ledge at the side of a sheltering cave – was probably early man's first seat, and the fact that many stones split naturally into manageable slabs along their bedding planes makes the construction of simple garden seating a relatively straightforward task.

The simplest structure, a bench, needs nothing more than a horizontal slab for the seat, resting on two or three securely-set supporting stones. Unless you are prepared for some laborious dressing work on the seat supports to ensure that the seat is level and will not rock, it makes sense to use cement mortar not only to bond the components together but also to take up any irregularity in their fit, effectively providing a

Right: A massive tabletop set on a stone drum is surrounded by a stone bench.

Below: A slate slab set on heavy stone blocks makes an unusual outdoor table.

Above: *Natural stone slabs set on sturdy legs create a sitting-out area with an eerily prehistoric look about it; only the stone trolls are missing.*

Left: *A little ingenuity is all it takes to turn even the most unlikely stone shapes into unusual garden seats.*

essential for bedding the stones and bonding the joints, and some additional reinforcement in the form of galvanised metal pins may be needed to give the seat extra strength.

Perhaps the most satisfying type of masonry seating to construct is a shelf seat and back slab built into a surrounding masonry wall. This acts as both back support and armrest, as well as supporting the seat itself, and the resulting structure combines the function of seat and wall in one potentially very attractive garden feature.

To build such a seat, you should plan the perimeter walls first. The structure is basically a masonry box; the front wall will support the front edge of the seat, the side walls will rise a little higher and act as armrests, while the back wall will rise to shoulder height and will support the angled back slabs. As the walls are built up, stones are set to project as corbels from the side and rear walls into the box level with the top of the front wall to provide supports for the seat

joint that can be compressed when the mortar is wet to ensure a level seat.

A variation on the simple bench seat is the cantilevered slab, built into a stone wall so that the seat projects from it at a comfortable height. The wall itself obviously needs to be fairly massive in width, since you need to set about one quarter of the slab (measured from front to back) within the wall structure to provide adequate

support to the slab. The additional weight of the rest of the wall, sitting on the rear edge of the seat slab, then helps to counteract the leverage imposed by someone sitting on the seat.

Slightly more elaborate is the slab seat – a bench with stone blocks set on it to form back and arm supports. Careful choice of the stone blocks used is essential if the seat is to be comfortable as well as structurally secure; mortar is

slabs. The side and rear walls are then built up to their required heights, and are topped off with capping stones to prevent rainwater from penetrating the wall structure.

Once the basic box has been completed, the next step is to use mortar to bed the seat slabs in place, resting their front edges on the top of the low front wall and setting their side and rear edges on the corbels built into the wall structure. Once the seat is in place, similar slabs can be added to form the back support. Set the slabs so that their lower edges rest on the seat slab, and lay them back at a slight angle so their top edges rest against the back wall. Use mortar to bond them in position and to point the gaps between both the seat and back slabs.

You can build a monumental seat of this sort as a straight bench, in a gentle curve or as a more steeply-curved horse-shoe shape, depending on its site.

The comfort factor

It must be said that unless a stone seat has been warmed up by standing in full sunlight for an hour or so, it is likely to be a cold and potentially rather damp place to sit. You can overcome this either by making individual slatted timber panels to suit each seat, or by making seat cushions. The former can obviously be left outside so long as they are made from preservative-treated timber, while the latter should be covered with waterproof fabric even if they are brought out only when they are required, to counteract any dampness in the stone. Latex foam is the ideal cushion filling for this situation, since it is itself moisture-resistant.

Building stone tables

Creating stone garden tables is really a variation on the simple bench principle. The basic ingredient is a single stone to act as the table top. This can either be a roughly-hewn and irregularly-shaped slab of sandstone or limestone, or a more highly-finished piece of slate or marble; it all depends on the visual effect you want to achieve and on what type of stone is most readily available locally.

To support the table top you have several options, each the masonry equivalent of tried-and-tested indoor furniture designs. One of the most spectacular is the centre pedestal, which works particularly well with the more massive and irregular table-top slabs. This is nothing more than a square block or a roughly cylindrical drum set on the ground to support the table top, which should be securely bedded on mortar to ensure that it cannot be toppled.

The second option is best for rectangular slabs, and involves setting the table top on two end supports – blocks or slabs set securely in the ground with their tops level ready to receive the table top.

The third option, more difficult to construct than the other two, requires the positioning of a sturdy stone column at each corner of the table. This method is ideal for supporting both square and rectangular table tops.

Using loose stone

There is obviously no substitute for large flat slabs when it comes to forming the working surfaces of garden seats and tables, but there is no reason why their supports should not be built up using small individual stones rather than more massive monoliths. This applies particularly to supports for tables, where you can build up end or corner supports as columns or panels of masonry bonded together with mortar. However, it is wise to incorporate some form of internal reinforcement within the supports to withstand lateral move-ment, since the table top itself is still likely to be fairly massive and a collapse of the supports could have serious consequences.

The best way of constructing such a support is to start by laying a shallow concrete foundation pad beneath the chosen support position. Then decide on the height of the support and prepare one or two steel reinforcing rods long enough to match this and to allow for the L-shaped end of the rod to be bedded in the concrete pad. Set the rods in the concrete immediately after placing it, and prop them upright while the concrete sets. You can then build up the masonry support round the reinforcing rod(s) to the required height, concealing them within the column or wall as you work. When you reach the top of the rod, add a generous pad of mortar on top of the pier and bed the table top in place.

Below: *Dressed slabs forming a flight of steps, a table and a bench have supports fashioned from contrasting stonework. The latter need internal reinforcement.*

PONDS

A POND IS ONE OF THE MOST ATTRACTIVE FEATURES YOU CAN CREATE IN YOUR GARDEN, BECAUSE IT BRINGS AN EXTRA DIMENSION: WATER. APART FROM PROVIDING A HOME FOR A COLLECTION OF ORNAMENTAL FISH, A POND ALLOWS YOU TO GROW A RANGE OF AQUATIC AND MARSH-LOVING PLANTS AND PROVIDES A NATURAL ATTRACTION FOR WILD LIFE OF ALL SORTS — BIRDS, AMPHIBIANS, INSECTS, EVEN THE OCCASIONAL CAT! BY SITING IT CAREFULLY, YOU CAN ALSO MAKE IT THE CENTREPIECE OF THE GARDEN, AND A SENSIBLE CHOICE OF SHAPE AND SIZE MEANS THAT IT WILL COMPLEMENT ANY GARDEN LAYOUT, FORMAL OR INFORMAL.

The one thing to remember about creating a pond is that it is more than just a construction job. While you can make a watertight hole in the ground and fill it with water almost overnight, the plants will take time to establish themselves and so it may take a season or two for the pond to become self-supporting. Once it has done so, however, it will be perfectly capable of looking after itself.

A CHOICE OF TYPES

The essential ingredient of any pond is a waterproof lining, and you can provide this in one of three common ways.

The simplest, if available, is a rigid pond liner. These are moulded from either reinforced glass fibre or PVC, and come in a wide range of shapes and sizes, up to a maximum of about 4 m (13

ft) long. Most are a neutral grey colour, but cream and blue are also available; some have edges moulded to resemble rocks or paving, while others need a natural stone surround to conceal their edges and help them to blend in with their surroundings. To install one, all you have to do is dig a hole of the right shape in the ground and lower the liner into place, checking that it is level and well supported with soil round the sides. A rigid liner is likely to be the most expensive type of pond; glass fibre types

Right: A raised pond, here built with natural stone and incorporated within a rockery, is the simplest type to build.

Below: Minimalist water gardening, with a small fountain cascading over a bed of cobbles within a semi-circular screen.

Above: *Incorporating a pond into your patio allows you to grow an attractive array of aquatic plants.*

cost a little more than PVC ones, but are stronger (although you should not stand in either type during installation or planting). Both can be repaired if they develop cracks, and should last for at least ten years.

A flexible liner placed in an in-ground excavation or within a retaining wall above ground is a better bet if you want a pond larger than the off-the-shelf sizes available in rigid liners, or if you want to create an unusual shape without too much hard work. The cheapest is 500-micron polythene, available in various shades and used as a double layer to line the excavation. This is easily punctured by stones, cats' claws and the like, virtually impossible to patch successfully and becomes brittle at the water line quite quickly because of the action of ultra-violet light in the sun's rays; expect a maximum life of three to five years. The maximum width of this type depends on its thickness.

PVC sheet is more expensive than polythene, but lasts on average about twice as long. Two types are available; ordinary liners have two layers of PVC

bonded together, while reinforced types have fabric mesh sandwiched between the two layers for extra strength. The PVC layers may be neutral or coloured. Various widths are available; larger sizes will have welded seams.

PVC sheet suffers from the same drawbacks as polythene; it is readily punctured (though reinforced types are fairly strong and holes in either type are easily mended with a vinyl repair kit), and it is also gradually degraded by sunlight. However, it makes a more natural-looking liner than polythene because the material stretches as the pond is filled, pulling out most of the creases and folds.

Butyl rubber is the most expensive type of liner available, but is by far the most durable; manufacturers claim a life of up to 50 years. It comes in black, charcoal grey and stone colours, and is highly resistant to puncturing (unless over-stretched) and degradation by sunlight.

The third type of liner you could choose is concrete. It is the best bet for large or ornately-shaped ponds, because large flexible liners can be very expensive. Obviously, using concrete means much more work than if a liner is fitted, and a lot of care has to be taken to make the pond waterproof. Even then,

leaks may occur due to soil shrinkage in summer, frost and ice damage in winter, even growing roots from nearby plants. It is therefore a good idea to line the hole with heavy-duty polythene first so that hairline cracks do not result in leaks, and to reinforce the concrete with metal mesh on large ponds.

Concrete ponds cannot be stocked immediately, since the lime in the mix is harmful to plants and fish. You have to neutralise this by filling and emptying the pond three times, leaving it to stand full for about a week each time. An alternative is to brush on a special neutralising agent, or to use a heavy-duty bituminous waterproofer (which also helps guard against leaks).

POND SIZE

The size of pond you construct depends largely on personal preference – and on the size restrictions noted above for individual pond types. It depends as much as anything on the size of your garden and on how large a feature you want the pond to be. In general terms, the bigger the pool can be, the better; tiny ponds not only look ridiculous, but they also tend not to develop into self-supporting life systems as well as larger ponds where nature quickly establishes a balance between plant life and the pond's inhabitants.

The only formal size guideline to bear in mind concerns the number of fish you plan to have. As a rough guide allow one square metre (11 sq ft) of surface area for every ten 50–75 mm (2–3 in) fish. If you are buying larger (and more expensive) fish, check the stocking level with your supplier.

POND SHAPE

Once you have settled on which type of pond you want to install, it is time to think about the shape. In a formal garden layout a square, rectangular or round pond usually looks best, while irregular shapes will suit an informal layout. Rigid liners come in regular and irregular shapes; if you are using a flexible liner you can drape it into almost any shape you want, but there will be unavoidable folds and overlaps at sharp internal corners.

With concrete, formal shapes are best cast in two stages; the base of the pond is laid first, and then plywood shuttering is set up to form a mould for the pond walls. These should be placed as soon as the base concrete is firm. The edges of the base should be keyed while the concrete is still wet to improve the bond between base and walls, and it is also a good idea to bed in some reinforcing mesh along the join as the base is laid. Informal pond shapes with sloping sides can be cast continuously or in stages, but again the joint between sections should be reinforced to prevent cracking.

ABOVE OR BELOW GROUND?

Most people automatically assume that a pond will be below ground, and one that sets out to imitate nature will obviously be installed in this way. But if you are creating a formal pond there is no reason why it should not be above ground, enclosed by raised retaining walls which can also incorporate other features such as planters, seats and steps, and could have a fountain or several levels linked by waterfalls. It is also worth considering this option in a garden designed for a disabled person, or where there is a danger of small children falling into a below-ground pond.

A variation on this idea involves setting the pond, perhaps again with a waterfall, into a raised bank or rockery. Such treatment certainly helps to make the pond even more of an eye-catching feature.

Right: *On sloping sites you have the opportunity to use running water, by pumping water to the top of the cascade from a holding pool at the bottom.*

CHOOSING THE SITE

Where your pond is sited is just as important as what it is made of or what shape it is. The main thing to avoid is shade, since this will prevent aquatic plants from developing properly. You should also steer clear of trees that drop their leaves, since they will clog up the pond every autumn and foul the water unless they are removed before they begin to decompose. The best position is one that will receive plenty of sunlight, yet is reasonably sheltered from any strong prevailing winds.

If you want to have lights round (or in) the pond, or plan to install a pump to run a fountain or waterfall, it is wise to consider a site fairly near to the house so the electricity supply is easy to install. You will then be able to enjoy the sight and sound of your pond from the house or patio, in the evening as well as during the day.

CARE AND MAINTENANCE

A well-balanced pond will look after itself for the most part, with a natural balance quickly establishing itself, keeping the water clear and the fish

PONDS

and plants healthy. As mentioned earlier, you will need to remove dead leaves and the like blown into the pond before they sink and decompose; it may be worth netting the pond in autumn to keep most debris out. If the water becomes murky, you can treat it with algicidal chemicals, available from pond equipment suppliers or pet shops; however, this is often just a passing phase, and it may clear of its own accord.

Cats (and birds in country areas) can be a menace, since both will poach fish. You can net the pond, but this rather detracts from its appearance. A better way of deterring cats is to surround the pond with a low ornamental wire fence of the type popular for edging flower beds; it needs to be no more than about 150mm (6in) high to keep them away. Herons wade into ponds to make their catch, so deny them access by netting the shallows or stringing black thread across it; the latter method has the advantage of being virtually invisible.

Ice is the fishes' biggest enemy in cold climates. If the pond is iced up for more than a day, gases from decomposing vegetation cannot escape and the fish may die. The best method of keeping at least part of the pool ice-free in cold weather is with a small pool heater. In no circumstances should the ice be broken by force, since this could stun or kill the fish; if you cannot keep a small ventilation opening clear with pans of boiling water or similar means, then it is better to leave any thick ice to thaw naturally.

Ice can also be a problem with steep-sided concrete pools, because the expansion across the surface can cause cracking. Avoid absolutely vertical sides if possible, since this allows the ice sheet to expand up the slope as it forms.

PROFESSIONAL ADVICE

The best places to visit for specialist advice about installing and managing a garden pond are water gardens suppliers. They can provide you with everything you need, from the pond itself to plants, fish, food, in-pond equipment such as planting containers, pumps and fountains, pond chemicals, repair kits and so on. Some also publish helpful leaflets and books on the subject, and are happy to deal with queries about any aspect of pond care.

BUILDING A CONCRETE POND

Ther are two particular circumstances in which concrete is the best choice for a garden pond. Firstly, you may want a formal-style pond in a shape or size that is not available as an off-the-shelf rigid liner. Secondly, your plan for a large free-form pond could mean having to buy a large very expensive liner; using concrete would be much cheaper.

The main drawbacks of using concrete are that your pond will take much longer to create (and you will not be able to stock it immediately unless you are prepared to seal the concrete surface in some way), and it may give more problems in the future than a rigid or flexible liner type.

Obviously, you can create any shape you want with concrete, but there are one or two practical limitations to take into consideration. If you plan a formal pond, you will need timber shuttering to support the sides of the pool, and this could be expensive

and difficult to set up for a large pond. If you are having an informal shape, you will have to be prepared to work fast in placing and finishing the concrete if potentially weak joins are to be avoided. Whichever type you choose, make sure that the central part of the pond is at least 400 mm (about 16 in) deep so it cannot freeze solid in winter; a deep end around 600 mm (2 ft) deep is ideal for fish to stay cool in hot weather. Use the shallows for plant containers.

THE CORRECT MIX

Concrete for a pond needs to be a fairly strong mix – 1 part cement to 1 part sharp sand and 2 parts coarse aggregate (or 1:3 if you are using all-in aggregate). For a job of this size it is well worth hiring a small concrete mixer; you will save time as well as effort. If you are planning to use ready-mixed concrete, your supplier will advise you on the best mix to use for the job. Make sure that you are equipped to shift the concrete quickly from where it has been tipped to the pond site so you can place it all before it starts to set.

Estimating quantities is easiest for a rectangular or other regular shape. The base and walls should be a minimum of 100 mm (4 in) thick, so you can work out the volume of the concrete one section at a time. With irregular-shaped bowls, estimate the area of the pond at ground level and double it to get the surface area of the bowl itself; then multiply this area by the thickness to arrive at an overall volume.

If you are mixing the concrete yourself, aim for a mix that is slightly on the

72

maker's instructions regarding coverage and number of coats.

Finish off the pond by bedding stone slabs or pavers all round the perimeter, and pointing the joints for a neat finish.

MAINTENANCE

The main problem with concrete ponds is that cracks can develop due to ground movement (more likely with rectangular types than free-form bowls, which tend to 'float' over subsidence like a boat). This means leaks, and all you can do if they occur is to empty the pond and patch them with a proprietary sealant or with mortar; in the latter case, rake out the cracks to at least 10 mm (⅜ in) wide so you can form a substantial repair, and coat the crack edges with PVA building adhesive or latex bonding agent first to improve the bond. Then re-apply a coat of pond sealer over the entire pond surface.

If the leaks persist or you cannot track them down, the best course of action is to empty the pond completely and fit a flexible liner inside the concrete shell.

Below: *Even the smallest pool can be given life by the addition of a pumped cascade and some low-level landscaping.*

dry side, especially if you are not using formwork. Too sloppy a mix will be difficult to place on sloping surfaces.

THE CONSTRUCTION

Once you have planned the shape and size of your pond and chosen its site, mark the outline with string and pegs and start digging. Remember to allow for the thickness of the concrete. With rectangular pools, cut the sides at an angle of about 20° to the vertical, and level the base.

If the subsoil is soft, put down a 100 mm (4 in) thick layer of well rammed hardcore in the base of the excavation, and blind it with sand. Otherwise, simply compact the base of the excavation thoroughly.

Lay a sheet of metal reinforcing mesh in the hole, covering just the base of a rectangular one, the whole of a free-form one. Cut and bend the mesh if necessary to get a good fit, and wire overlapping sections together.

Pour the concrete. In a rectangular pond, cast the base slab first, and check that it is level and well compacted. With a free-form pond, start in the centre (1) and build up the concrete layer round the pond sides. Work from a scaffold board spanning the pond.

With rectangular ponds, add reinforcement round the sides and erect the formwork for the sides using shuttering plywood and softwood braces. Check carefully that the shuttering is level; once the pool is filled, any errors will be glaringly obvious.

Pour the concrete into the formwork and tamp it down well. Finish it off level with the top of the formwork, and add the ledge all round which will support the perimeter paving. Float the concrete smooth in a free-form pond, then cover the concrete with polythene sheeting so it cannot dry out too quickly.

Next, add features such as small top feeder pools (2) and waterfalls (3), and finish the concrete surface with coloured rendering if you wish (4).

Where formwork has been used, remove it after about 14 days and apply a 25 mm (1 in) thick 1:3 mortar render over the pool sides and base. Add a waterproofer to the mix as an extra safeguard.

Before adding plants or fish, condition or seal the concrete to remove the harmful lime from the surface. Conditioning means filling the pool, leaving it to stand for two or three days and then emptying it again; repeat this twice more. Alternatively, brush on a proprietary pond sealer, following the

Constructing a liner pond

Flexible liners offer the easiest, quickest and most adaptable way of creating a garden pond; all you need is a hole in the ground – or a retaining wall structure if you want an above-ground pond – and a liner big enough to fill it.

Planning

Before you can work out how big a liner you need, you have to decide on the site, style and shape of your pond. Most people simply dig a hole in the lawn, but you may prefer to create a raised pond – either an informal one, perhaps within a rockery, or a formal one surrounded by masonry walls and a parapet. You will need a combination of hole in the ground and retaining wall on sloping sites.

For in-ground ponds, the simplest way of planning the position and shape is to use rope or the garden hose (1). Lay it out and move it around until you get the shape you want; then check how it will look from further away by viewing it from an upstairs window.

For raised ponds you will have to carry out some or all of the preliminary construction work first. The big advantage of this type of pond is that you are working mainly above ground level, so there is less stooping involved, and with walled types you can conceal the edges of the liner neatly beneath the final course of capping.

At the planning stage, you should also think about the depth of the pond. This should be a minimum of 380 mm (15 in) for the smallest ponds, increasing to 450 mm (18 in) for ponds with a surface area of between 2.5 and 9 sq m (25 and 100 sq ft) and to 600 mm (24 in) for areas up to 20 sq m (220 sq ft). Remember that these are recommendations for the deep centre of the pond; if you want marginal plants, you can have shallower shelves round the pond perimeter.

Measuring up

Most manufacturers of pool liners use a standard formula for finding the size of liner you need. The length is the overall pond length plus twice the maximum depth, the width the overall pond width plus twice the maximum depth. Because of the stretchiness of the sheeting, no extra allowance is needed for the overlap round the perimeter. So a pond 3 x 2 m (10 ft x 6 ft 6 in) in size and 450 mm (18 in) deep will need a 4 x 3 m (13 x 10 ft) liner.

Other materials

Unless your subsoil is relatively free from stones, you should line the pond excavation with a cushioning layer of sand about 25 mm (1 in) thick. A cubic metre (1.3 cu yd) of sand will cover about 37 sq m (400 sq ft) to this thickness.

In addition, you may like to ensure the longest possible life for your new pond by laying special fabric matting over the sand bed before fitting the liner itself. This is generally 2 m (6 ft 6in) wide, and is simply draped into the excavation and overlapped at the joins.

For an in-ground pond, you can simply turf up to the edge... so long as you do not mind fishing grass cuttings out of the water every time you mow the lawn. It is better to provide a paved area surrounding the pond, so you will need some suitable slabs, plus sand and cement for bedding and pointing them.

For raised pools with perimeter walls, or ponds with retaining walls above and below on sloping sites, you will need concrete for strip foundations as well as suitable stone or garden walling blocks (plus mortar) for the walls themselves.

Building a liner pond

With your pond outline marked and your liner delivered, you are ready to start work on the actual installation.

Clear turf and other vegetation from the pond site, and start excavating it (2). Save topsoil in one heap (on a tarpaulin or boards so you do not spoil the lawn) for use elsewhere in the garden, and dispose of the subsoil separately – either by using it to create a raised garden feature, or by having it taken away.

Work out towards the pond edges, forming a flat base to the excavation and sloping the sides at an angle of about 20° as you near the edge (3). Cut planting shelves as required, making them about 230 mm (9 in) wide and

230 mm or so below the final water level. Finally, cut back the turf at the pond edge as necessary to accommodate the edge paving.

Complete the final shaping of the excavation, and carefully remove any sharp stones protruding from the sides or base. Then cover the base and sides with a 25 mm (1 in) thick layer of damp sand (4) to act as a cushion and protect the liner from punctures. Pat it into place, and also use it to fill any holes left by prising out sharp stones.

Check that the pool edge is precisely level by driving short wooden pegs into the plateau where the paving will go, and holding a spirit level across them (use a long straightedge if

Right: *The finished pond, complete with oxygenating plants and submerged planters, ready for the fish to arrive.*

PONDS

Right: Even the smallest garden has room for a pond. Here, a simple raised version adjoins a matching patio.

you have only a short level). Remove or add soil as necessary. If you do not do this, the filled pond will show up any high spots.

Drape the liner loosely into the hole (after laying fabric matting, if you have decided to use it). Aim for an even overlap all round. Then anchor the overlap at intervals with stones to ensure that the liner stretches evenly as you fill it with water.

Start running the water in (5), easing off the stones to ensure that the liner fits snugly as the water level rises. Some creasing is inevitable, but you can smooth out major creases by hand as they occur.

Once the pool is full, you can go round the perimeter and cut off the liner

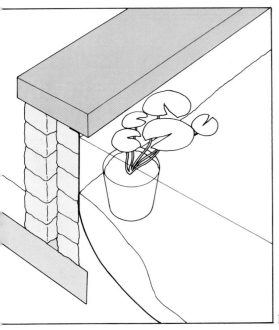

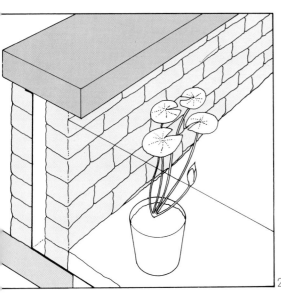

1

overlap (6), leaving about 150 mm (6 in) all round to lie on the perimeter plateau. Save some small offcuts in case you need to patch a puncture in the liner at any time in the future.

Lay the perimeter paving on a generous bed of mortar so that it overlaps the pond edge by about 50 mm (2 in), and point the joints (7). Where lawn adjoins the paving, set the slabs with their surface just below ground level so you will not damage the mower blades. Top up the pool so that the final water level is about 25 mm (1 in) below the under-

side of the overhanging slabs, so that the area of liner exposed to view (and to potentially damaging sunlight) is kept to an absolute minimum.

Leave the pond to stand for a few days before introducing the plants, and give these (especially the vital oxygenating ones) time to become established before finally adding the fish.

BUILDING A RAISED POND

Whether you are building a complete perimeter wall or just a short retaining

2

one, you need proper foundations to ensure that it stays where you put it. The technique is the same as for building any garden wall.

You can build these walls in one of two ways – as a single thickness of masonry with the liner draped inside it (1), or as a double-skinned construction with the inner skin added once the liner has been installed (2). The advantage of the latter method is that the liner is invisible at the sides of the pond – all you see is the attractive masonry – and so is less prone to accidental damage or degradation by the weather.

Plan the position, size and shape of the pond carefully, and excavate the trenches for the foundation concrete. Place this and leave it to harden for at least 48 hours.

If the pond is to be half-raised, excavate the deeper central portion at this stage, leaving the plant shelf at roughly the same level as the foundation concrete. Remove stones, and lay a sand cushion as with in-ground ponds.

Build up the perimeter or retaining walls as per your design, checking carefully as you build that each course is precisely level – vital with a complete perimeter wall. When you reach the final height, check the levels again. Allow the mortar to harden for 48 hours before fitting the liner. With a raised pond, lay a sand cushion over the base of the 'hole'.

Lay the liner in place, with an even overlap all round, and with a square or rectangular pond form neat 'hospital corner' folds at each internal angle. Anchor the liner with stones placed on top of the wall.

If you are using the concealed liner technique mentioned earlier, build up the inner leaf of masonry now, working from outside the pool if possible so you do not risk puncturing the liner by standing on it. Check the coursing as the wall rises; its last course should obviously be

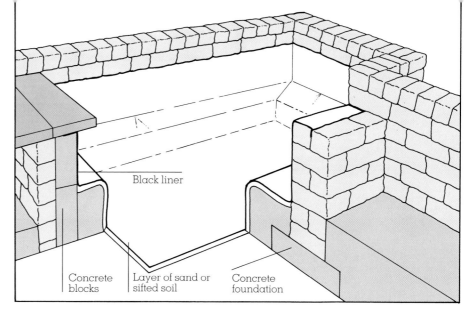

Black liner

Concrete blocks | Layer of sand or sifted soil | Concrete foundation

level with the outer wall. Neaten the pointing and remove any mortar droppings.

Fill the liner with water, easing off the anchor stones and neatening the internal corner folds as the water level rises. When it is full, trim off the overlap all round, leaving a flap about half the masonry width in size to be covered by the capping stones.

Finish off by laying the capping stones in place to secure the edges of the liner, and top up the pond so the water level is just below the underside of the overhang.

With the double-skin type, empty and refill the pond a couple of times to get rid of the alkalinity caused by the mortar pointing. Then introduce first the plants, then the fish, just as for in-ground ponds.

OTHER WATER FEATURES

The traditional way of creating moving water in the garden is to install a fountain or waterfall in an existing garden pond. However, if you do not have a pond or your garden is not big enough for one, you can still enjoy the pleasures of a water feature in a very small space.

The secret is to create a miniature version of a full-scale pond-and-fountain installation. All you need is a reservoir (usually at or just below ground level) to supply the water, a small pump to circulate it and some hosepipe or small-diameter tubing to connect everything up and complete the circuit. The water can emerge by overflowing from a container of some sort (perhaps an ornamental urn, a pre-cast concrete birdbath or a wall-mounted gargoyle), from a fountain head or from a free-standing decorative garden ornament such as a spouting dolphin. It then runs down and is collected in the reservoir, from where it is simply recycled by the pump back to its discharge point. The whole system is self-contained, so you will not get a waterlogged garden and you will simply need to top it up occasionally to replace losses from evaporation and spray.

Many water garden suppliers now offer a range of these water features, ready for you to install. All they need is a power supply to run the pump. The simplest have a reservoir that stands above ground, like a planter, and are filled with large pebbles in the middle of which a small fountain discharges. Larger versions feature centrepieces such as imitation millstones (with the water discharging upwards through the centre hole in the stone), or ornate fountain centrepieces which often do double duty as a birdbath. Both types are designed to stand within a ground-level or above-ground reservoir.

If you prefer to create your own water feature, you can do so by combining your own choice of cascade, fountain or other discharge point with an in-ground or above-ground reservoir. This can be a flexible liner or a rigid moulded pool, and can be left as 'open water' or filled with pebbles, just like the ready-made water features mentioned above. If the feature is to be above ground, it is a simple matter to form a support for the liner in much the same way as building a raised planter.

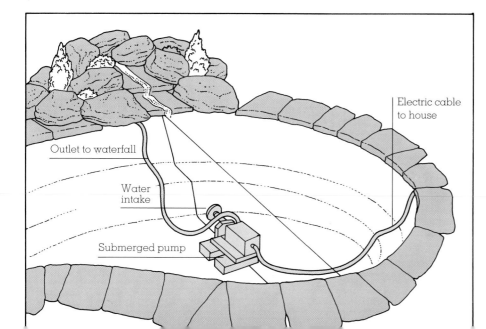

Outlet to waterfall

Water intake

Submerged pump

Electric cable to house

SMALL WEEKEND PROJECTS

THIS FINAL SECTION LOOKS AT SOME OF THE SMALLER-SCALE PROJECTS YOU CAN TACKLE. YOU MAY WANT TO CARRY THEM OUT TO ADD THE FINAL TOUCHES TO A LARGE OUTDOOR STONEWORK PROJECT, OR JUST TO EMBELISH YOUR GARDEN WITH A FEW SIMPLE DECORATIVE FEATURES. ALL ARE QUICK TO CONSTRUCT AND REQUIRE LITTLE IN THE WAY OF EXPENSIVE MATERIALS, BUT WILL ENHANCE ANY GARDEN IN WHICH THEY ARE SITED.

MOUNTING A SUNDIAL

One of the most attractive small stone features you can add to your garden is a sundial. Apart from being a pleasing object in its own right, it will provide an amusing diversion on sunny days and will be an object of fascination for children used to telling the time from more technologically sophisticated time-keeping equipment.

The essential ingredients of a sundial are the clock face and the style or gnomon (the pointer that casts the shadow that tells the time). There is nothing to stop you from making these yourself, using trial and error to get the hour spacings correct on the dial; set the pointer at an angle to the dial equal to the degree of latitude where you live. However, it will be simpler and quicker to buy a ready-made dial – they are sometimes available in a variety of metallic and cast resin finishes – and to set it on a column and base of your own design.

The sundial shown here consists of four pieces of stone. The pedestal is formed from two square slabs, one smaller than the other, with smooth top and bottom surfaces and roughly dressed edges. The column is a slightly tapered rough-dressed pillar set on the pedestal, and the dial support is an octagon – a square with the corners cut off at 45° – again with smooth top and bottom surfaces and rough-dressed edges all round. The dial itself can be surface-mounted on the support or set in a shallow circular recess ground into the stone.

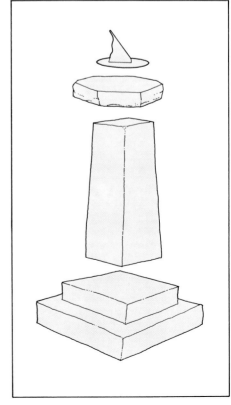

PAVING AROUND TREES

There will often be situations where you want to lay paving of one sort or another in an area already occupied by a specimen tree or two. If you are to avoid depriving the tree's roots of air and water, it is obviously out of the question to take the paving right up to the trunk itself. One solution is to lay the paving units up to a point no closer than about 300 mm (12 in) from the trunk depending on the size of the tree, with a slight slope to encourage rainwater to run into the roots, and then lay cobbles around the trunk to help discourage weeds from growing. Bed the slabs on sand, not mortar.

Stepping stones and water go well together too. If you are lucky enough to have a stream running through your garden, or you have a largish pond, then stepping stones can allow you to cross the water and continue your path. With a pond, they also make access for pond maintenance – trimming the lilies or thinning out oxygenating weed, for example – easier and safer.

CHOOSING MATERIALS

You can use any flat paving material for your stepping stones. Reconstituted stone or concrete slabs – the sort widely used for patios and garden paths – are ideal. They come in squares, rectangles, hexagons and circles, so you can use them for formal or informal arrangements, and colours range from yellows and buffs to red, green and grey.

Left: *A line of small stepping stones set in the lawn is unobtrusive, and keeps feet dry in wet weather.*

Below: *Make sure that individual stones are set low in the ground so that they do not catch on lawnmower blades.*

LAYING STEPPING STONES

You can use stepping stones in a number of different ways as an alternative to the traditional garden path. For example, a series of stones could run across the lawn – to the shed or greenhouse, for example, or to a focal point such as a seat or birdbath – and will allow traffic even in wet weather when the lawn is soft and sodden. The shapes of the individual stones, and the way in which they are arranged, allows you to create a straight and formal effect or a meandering, almost natural one.

There is another obvious advantage of having stepping stones instead of a continuous path: cost. If you need to provide a lengthy footway in your garden, continuous paving of any sort could prove quite expensive, while a few stepping stones will, literally, go a long way.

You can also use stepping stones in conjunction with other materials. For example, a path created from individual stones surrounded by cobbles, shingle or crushed bark looks most attractive, and is inexpensive to lay and easy to maintain.

Another use for stepping stones is to provide easier access within wide borders and flowerbeds. It is impossible to reach plants and shrubs at the back of the bed without compacting the soil, whereas a few strategically-placed stones could solve the problem and save you from getting muddy feet when gardening.

Natural stone looks even better – literally, more natural in appearance, as though the line of stones just 'happened' instead of being put there by man. The most common types are granites, limestones and sandstones, which range in colour from grey to a warm buff yellow and even red, and which can be readily split along the 'grain' into randomly-textured slabs. Larger boulders are ideal for use in ponds or flowerbeds. Slate can also look extremely attractive, but can be slippery when wet unless 'riven' stones with a rough surface are selected.

Laying stones across a lawn

This is the simplest way of laying stones, since they are held in position by the surrounding turf.

Start by planning out the line of the path across the lawn, using pieces of cardboard cut from grocery boxes as imitation stones. With these, you can experiment with both the line the path will take and the best spacing of individual stones before spending any money. You can also count up precisely how many stones you will need.

Mark the chosen stone positions with small wooden pegs, pushed into the lawn surface. Three pegs per stone are sufficient to do this accurately.

When the stones arrive, have a dry run by simply laying them out on the lawn surface. You can check the appearance of the path best from an upstairs window, with a helper in the garden to make any last-minute adjustments that may be needed to the layout.

Use a small border spade or a turf edging tool to cut neatly round the perimeter of each stone to a depth slightly more than the stone's thickness. Then set the stone to one side, and lift the turf. Save it; it may come in useful for repairs to worn patches and crumbling edges elsewhere on the lawn.

Remove any large stones and roots from the hole, and sieve some soil or builders' sand into the bottom to a depth of about 25 mm (1 in). This will make it easier to bed the stone in place firmly and prevent it from rocking when stepped on.

Lay the stone in place, and tamp it down – either use a baulk of timber such as a fence post off-cut, or simply jump up and down on it. Check that it sits level, with its top just below the soil surface, so you will be able to mow the grass without the mower blades clipping the edges of the stone. If necessary, lift the stone and add or remove soil until you are happy with the level.

Finish by trickling soil into any gaps round the edges of the stone, or use off-cuts of turf if you badly over-cut the hole to begin with. Then lay the rest of the stones in the same way.

Laying stones across a pond or stream

The task of positioning the stones is a little more difficult here, since safety is of paramount importance.

First of all, measure the depth of the water in which your stones will be set, and find out what surface they will rest on. In natural ponds and streams the bottom will be soil or gravel; in a man-made pond you may find concrete, plastic or rubber sheeting or rigid plastic. It is best not to lay stones on flexible pond liners, since you may puncture and crack them, but concrete is fine.

Work out what sort of stones to buy. For a formal pond setting, paving slabs are probably the likeliest choice; they will be set on a built-up brick or stone plinth so their surface is just above water level. For a more natural effect in reasonably shallow ponds and streams, choose individual boulders with relatively flat top and bottom surfaces, thick enough to project about 50 mm (2 in) above the water level.

With natural ponds and streams, you can simply set the stones in place on the bottom. Use a trowel to excavate a shallow hollow, and set each stone in place. If it is too low, scoop soil back into the hollow. Then pack more soil round the sides of the stone to help keep it in place. If you want to ensure that the stone will not move, drive metal pegs in all round it, with their heads below water level. Use non-ferrous metal if possible (aluminium tent pegs are ideal); rust will discolour pond water.

With man-made concrete ponds, you need to lower the water level so that you can build up the plinth or position the boulder on 'dry' land (you are unlikely to be setting the stepping stones in the deepest part of the pond, so you will not have to disturb the fish). Simply siphon the water out with a length of garden hose; remember to remove it when the level has dropped sufficiently, or it will continue siphoning and you will end up with an empty pond.

Now build up a plinth for each paving slab, using engineering-quality bricks or garden walling blocks and mortar made with a waterproofing additive. For a slab 450 mm (18 in) square, you need a plinth about 350 mm (14 in) square – four bricks per course, laid in herringbone fashion. Build the plinth up to roughly the normal water level, then bed the stepping stone on top. Neaten up the pointing and leave it to harden for at least 48 hours before refilling the pond.

If you are using boulders, simply set stones of the right thickness on a mortar bed laid on the pond bottom – again after lowering the water level as necessary. You can use slate or tile to pack the level up if necessary. Finish off with a collar of mortar round the base of the stone.

Right: *Use small stepping stones set in a pond or stream to allow safe access to other parts of the garden.*

1

3

BUILDING A PATIO PLANTER

Another attractive weekend stonework project is the construction of a low-level patio planter. You can set it on any firm paved surface; the structure is light enough not to need full-scale foundations, making it ideal for any situation.

You can use natural stone if it is available, or man-made garden walling blocks otherwise; there is a variety of man-made blocks that could have been tailor-made for a project such as this. Each 'block' has its faces and ends moulded to resemble a section of dry-stone walling, and all you have to do is build up the structure to the required extent and height by bedding the blocks on bricklaying mortar and pointing the joints to match the recesses between the moulded stones. To finish off the wall,

2

4

use capping blocks moulded to look like the traditional on-edge stones used on dry-stone walls.

1 Work out the size of planter you want to build, and order the required number of walling and capping blocks. You will also need cement and soft sand (or premixed dry-pack bricklaying mortar), plus a brick bolster and club hammer to cut the blocks, a shovel for mixing the mortar, and a bricklaying trowel and spirit level for laying the blocks.

2 Start by laying the blocks that form the first course of the planter, setting them on a mortar bed and checking that they are level. There is no need to point the vertical courses, though you can if you wish.

3 Add the second course, changing the bonding pattern of the blocks as shown to give the wall additional strength.

4 When you have completed the planter walls, add the capping stones, setting them on a narrow ribbon of mortar along the centre line of the walling blocks for extra strength. Tap each block down so it is level.

5 You will probably have to cut one or two of the capping stones to length to complete the planter. Set the block on a bed of sand and use your brick bolster and club hammer to split the block at the desired position. It should break cleanly along the plane between the individual moulded stones.

6 Complete the planter by setting the cut length of capping stone in place. Then leave the mortar to harden for 48 hours before filling the planter with soil and compost, ready for planting.

Right: The finished planter, filled with compost and planted out with variegated ivy and colourful bedding plants.

REFERENCE

THIS CLOSING SECTION CONTAINS ADDITIONAL INFORMATION ABOUT THE TOOLS AND MATERIALS YOU WILL NEED FOR THE OUTDOOR STONEWORK PROJECTS DESCRIBED EARLIER IN THE BOOK. IT ALSO SUMMARISES THE MAIN TECHNIQUES INVOLVED, INCLUDING CLEARING AND PREPARING SITES, WORKING WITH CONCRETE AND CUTTING BLOCKS AND SLABS.

BASIC BUILDING TOOLS

You will need a selection of basic tools for jobs such as clearing, excavating and levelling sites, setting out projects, mixing, placing mortar and concrete, and so on.

The basic excavation tools are a pickaxe and a shovel. The pickaxe has a pointed tip at one end of its curved blade which is used for hacking into and breaking up solid masonry or old concrete, and a spade-ended tip at the other end for grubbing out loose materials so they can be dug out with the shovel. The pickaxe is available with a range of different head weights, commonly 2.2, 3 and 4.5 kg (5, 6½ and 10 lb), and has a strong hardwood handle about 900 mm (36 in) long.

If you are demolishing walls or breaking up concrete, you may find a sledgehammer a useful alternative to the pickaxe. This has a squared-off head weighing anything from 3.2 to 6.3 kg (7 to 14 lb), and a handle up to 900 mm (36 in) long, similar to the pickaxe.

If you have a lot of demolition work to do or have to break up thick concrete, hiring an electric breaker may speed up the process and save a lot of effort. Breakers are available with a range of inter-changeable cutting points (chipping points) and chisels.

The shovel, available with either a rounded or squared-off blade, is better than a spade for shifting loose material since the slightly raised sides help retain material on the blade. However, a spade will also be useful for a wide range of general digging, levelling and other site preparation work.

A tool that is valuable for moving heavy weights, whether you are lifting or placing heavy stone blocks, is the straight crowbar. This is a long steel rod with a point at one end and a chisel blade at the other; to use it you place one end under the object to be moved, position a sturdy fulcrum such as a block of masonry under the bar as close to the loaded end as possible, and apply downward pressure on the other end.

It is likely that you will have to move sizeable amounts of soil, rubble, concrete and stone during the construction of whatever you are creating. It is well worth buying or hiring a sturdy steel contractor's wheelbarrow with a pneumatic tyre; you will soon wreck an ordinary garden wheelbarrow, especially when moving heavy pieces of stone. Make sure you also have a supply of stout planks (scaffold boards are ideal) for use as runways and ramps if you are working on soft or broken ground, to prevent the barrow's wheel from becoming bogged down.

If your project calls for large quantities of mortar or concrete, hire a small electric concrete mixer for the duration of the job. This will save a lot of back-breaking hand mixing, and will also ensure that the mortar or concrete is evenly and thoroughly mixed to the required consistency.

TOOLS FOR SETTING OUT

The basic requirements here are pegs and stringlines, a steel tape measure and a builder's square. Make up a supply of tapered sawn timber pegs about 300 mm (12 in) long, and saw a notch all round each one just below its top to help retain the strings as you set out your site.

You can make up an accurate builder's square using three lengths of sawn or planed wood. Cut one about 1 m (3 ft 3 in) long and another about 1.3 m (4 ft 3 in) long, and connect them at right angles using a halving joint. Then cut the third piece about 1.6 m (5 ft 3 in) long, and nail it across the other two pieces to form a triangle. Cut off the excess wood from the ends of the angled length.

If you are building dry-stone walls, you will need a home-made device called a batter frame to act as a guide. This consists of four lengths of wood nailed together in a gently-tapered A-shape, with its dimensions selected to match the wall height and its projected thickness at the base and top. It carries movable string-lines that are raised as the wall is built up to keep the wall faces on line.

When it comes to levelling sites, an ordinary spirit level (see BEDDING TOOLS below) is of little use. More versatile is a water level, a length of hosepipe with pieces of clear plastic tube inserted into the ends. The hose is filled with water and corked at each end. Then the tubes are tied to pegs driven into the ground and the corks are removed; the water level in the tubes indicates the true horizontal at each end of the hose.

BEDDING TOOLS

You will need a bricklaying trowel if you are working with mortar, whether bedding stones in a wall or laying slabs in a mortar bed. You can use its handle for tamping blocks and slabs into place, but you will find a club hammer better at this; it is also needed for cutting and shaping blocks and slabs, in conjunction with your cutting tools (see below).

The other essential tool for this stage of the work is a spirit level, to ensure that blocks and slabs are laid truly level. Choose a long metal level for accuracy, and make sure it has end vials to indicate true vertical as well.

CUTTING TOOLS

The basic tool for cutting blocks and slabs is the brick chisel or bolster. It is made of steel, measures about 180 mm (7 in) long overall, and has a cutting edge 55 to 100 mm ($2\frac{1}{2}$ to 4 in) wide which is ground on both edges. It is held at right angles to the material being cut, and is struck with a club hammer.

The latter, sometimes known as the lump hammer, is a scaled-down relative of the sledgehammer, and has a similar squared-off head weighing up to 1.8 kg (4 lb). It is used for driving carving tools (see below) as well.

An alternative to the club hammer for driving masonry chisels and bolsters is the brick hammer. This has a slightly curved head with a square driving face at one end, and a sharp chisel blade at the other, which is useful for hand-trimming cut edges after the block or slab has been cut.

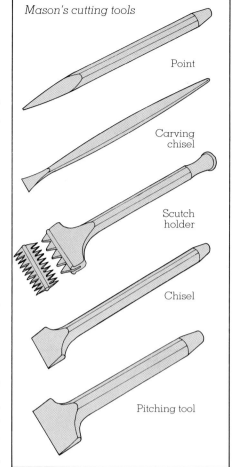

Mason's cutting tools

Point

Carving chisel

Scutch holder

Chisel

Pitching tool

CARVING TOOLS

For carving stone as opposed to just cutting it, you will need some special mason's carving tools (and a club hammer to drive them). The basic cutting and shaping tool is a chisel, an all-steel construction with a hexagonal cross-section and a square-ended cutting blade; it is available in sizes ranging from 12 to 50 mm ($\frac{1}{2}$ to 2 in) wide. The point chisel or punch, as its name implies, has a pointed cutting tip, and is used to concentrate the force of the hammer on a small area of the stone during the initial roughing-out of the workpiece. The pitching tool has a wide single-ground blade, and is used for removing larger amounts of stone when trimming a workpiece down to the required size.

For carving recesses, the most versatile tool of all is a mason's scutch holder, a special chisel-like tool with a replaceable cutting edge known as a scutch. This is double-sided, and may have plain or toothed edges. It is used after the initial roughing-out, and the toothed version leaves a series of furrows in the stone which can either be left as the final finish or can be smoothed off using either the plain mason's chisel or the wider mason's bolster.

Building tools you will need include:
A spirit level (1), a brick bolster (2), a cold chisel (3), walling pegs (4), a stringline (5), walling line blocks (6), a club hammer (7), a bricklaying trowel (8), a pointing trowel (9), and a hawk (10).

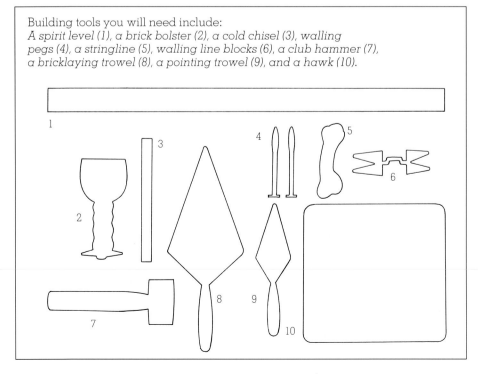

Natural stone

The main stones used for outdoor projects fall into one of three classes: igneous, sedimentary and metamorphic. Igneous rocks were formed by the cooling of molten magma, while sedimentary stones were created either by the wearing down of older rocks or from accumulations of organic origin.

Metamorphic stones are stones that have been changed structurally from their original form by immense heat and pressure.

Granite is the commonest igneous stone. It is extremely dense and hard (and therefore expensive to quarry and cut), highly resistant to attack by pollution, and is almost impervious to water penetration. This makes it ideal for use as a paving material – usually in the form of small blocks called setts – and for areas getting heavy wear, such as steps and kerbs. Most granites are grey or black, but there are also varieties with green, red, pink or blue colouring, caused by the inclusion of felspar or other minerals.

The sedimentary stones are by far the most widely used for outdoor stonework projects. They fall into two broad groups, the sandstones and the limestones. Sandstones consist mainly of particles of quartz, bound together by other minerals such as silica and carbonates and often contain iron ores which help to give the stone its attractive colouring. This can range from almost white to red, brown and even blue-grey. The best sandstones are very durable, but as a type they tend to weather less attractively than the limestones and some can quickly become soiled by atmospheric pollution. Their most popular use is as split flagstones.

Limestones consist mainly of calcium carbonate (calcite), and were formed in one of three ways. Most of the building limestones are known as oolitic stones,

Top: *If you are lucky enough to live near a quarry, this will prove an invaluable source of supplies for your projects.*

Left: *Otherwise, you will have to rely on the smaller stocks of stone held by many builders' merchants and garden centres.*

and were formed by the accretion of calcite round small grains of sand or shell, these then being cemented together by more calcite. Limestones were also formed by deposition – the accumulation of organic remains such as shells and other animal or plant remains – or by crystallization from solution (stalactites and stalagmites, for example). They vary widely in hardness, although as a group they are generally softer and easier to work than sandstones, making them ideal for carving as well as for more general building work. They are, however, attacked by acid rain which initially makes the surface self-cleaning but which in the longer term can cause rapid decay of the softer types. Colours range from creamy white (Portland-stone, for example) to light brown.

Since both sandstones and limestones were formed in layers, they have distinct bedding planes which should be reproduced in any structure built with them; they will gradually delaminate if laid with the bedding plane parallel to an exposed face of a wall, for example.

The most common metamorphic stone is slate, formed from heated and compressed clay – a process that turned limestone into marble and sandstone into quartzite. This process resulted in a stone that has distinct planes of cleavage, often almost at right angles to the original bedding planes, along which the stone can be split to form slabs of varying thickness. It is strong in tension and compression and has good resistance to moisture penetration, although some types are attacked by acidic pollution, and can be used in blocks as well as slabs for a variety of end uses.

As mentioned earlier in the book, your choice of stone for garden projects is likely to depend on what local suppliers stock unless you live close to quarries and can specify your requirements more precisely. You will also be in your supplier's hands as far as selecting stone in the size, shape and finish you want. Stone surfaces are classified according to the degree of finish they have been subjected to. The most common terms, in increasing order of

Below: *Examples of the wide range of colour and surface texture available, especially in the sandstones and lmestones that are the most popular materials for most stonework projects. If possible, choose stone that matches existing features in your garden.*

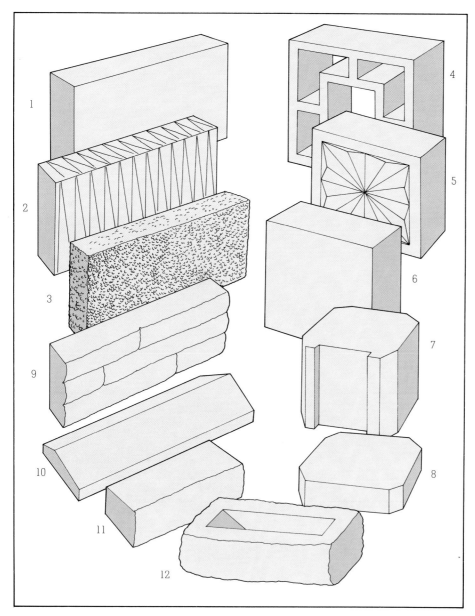

Left: *Man-made concrete blocks: Solid dense concrete (1), Lightweight aerated (2), Lightweight aggregate (3), Pierced decorative (4), Solid decorative (5), Pitched-face reconstituted stone (6), Pilaster block (7), Pilaster coping (8), Multi-stone block (9), Screen coping (10), Split-face facing (11), Hewn-stone facing (12).*

– an actual size of 290 mm (11⅜ in) square and about 90 mm (3½ in) thick, giving a work size of 300 mm (11¾ in) square. You need 11 blocks per square metre of wall. Coping stones, if available, usually come in 610 mm (2 ft) lengths – long enough to bridge two of the walling blocks and three 10 mm (⅜ in) mortar joints. The special hollow pier blocks that some manufacturers make as part of their screen walling block range are about 200 mm (8 in) square and 190 mm (7½ in) tall. Allowing for a 10 mm mortar joint, this means that three pier blocks build up to the same height – 600 mm or just under 2 ft – as two walling blocks.

PAVING SLABS AND BLOCKS

Reconstituted stone paving slabs are mostly squares or rectangles, and come in a range of sizes based on a 225 mm, 250 mm, 300 mm or 500 mm (9, 10, 12 or 20 in) module. The largest manageable size is 675 x 450 mm (27 x 18 in). To estimate roughly how many slabs will be needed for a particular project, divide the area to be paved by the area of an individual slab. In practice, however, it is better to design paved areas if possible so they are a whole number of slabs wide and long, to minimise the need for cutting slabs. Then you can count how many rows there are and how many slabs are needed in each row, and multiply the two figures. If you are laying mixed slabs of different sizes, draw a scale plan on squared paper and count how many of each size will be required.

Some paving ranges also include hexagonal and circular slabs. The former are usually 400 mm (16 in) wide, measured between two opposite parallel sides, and come with matching straight-sided half slabs to allow you to pave square or rectangular areas with them. You will need 55 x 400 mm hexagonal slabs to pave an area of 10sq m (108sq ft). Circular slabs come in several diameters from 300 mm (12 in) upwards, and are intended to be laid as individual stepping stones.

Cast concrete slabs – the cheapest type – are usually 50 mm (2 in) thick, while the more expensive reconstituted stone types are generally 40 mm (1⅝ in) thick. They are surprisingly heavy – a 450 mm (18 in) sq slab weighs around 16 kg (36 lbs) – so lift them with care.

Block pavers are generally rectangular, although there are some made in

smoothness, are: rockfaced; rough picked; fair picked; axed; fine axed; split (riven); sawn or ribbed; sanded; gritted; honed or rubbed; polished (unlikely to be required in the garden). As far as quantities are concerned, give as much detail of the project you are tackling as possible and take your supplier's advice.

MAN-MADE WALL BLOCKS

Reconstituted stone blocks, made to imitate natural stone, come in a wide range of sizes. The most common measure from 200 to 325 mm (8¼ to 12¾ in) long, 75 to 150 mm (3¼ to 5¾ in) wide and 65 to 150 mm (2¾ to 5¾ in) high – the same height as a standard brick. Others in the range are usually multiples of this, which allows you to lay the blocks in a wide range of decorative bonds.

In some countries you may also find larger blocks which have their outer face moulded so they resemble a number of smaller, randomly-shaped blocks. The moulded joints are deeply recessed, and each block may have projecting units at each end to allow a stretcher-style bond to be achieved between neighbouring blocks. The result is a stronger wall than could be built with simple stack bonding.

To estimate the quantities you will need for a particular project, first select the block you want to work with and then use its actual size as a guide. To work out how many blocks will be required for one square metre (11sq ft) of single-thickness masonry, add 10 mm (⅜ in) to the actual block length and height (in mm) to allow for the thickness of the mortar joint, multiply the two figures together, and divide the result into 1,000,000 (the number of sq mm in a sq m). So, for a 440 x 65 mm block, the sum is: 450 x 75 = 33,750 sq mm, then 1,000,000 divided by 33,750 = 29.63, which means you need 30 blocks per sq m.

Perforated decorative screen walling blocks are made in just one standard size

inter-locking shapes to give a less regular look to the surface of the paved area. The standard block size is 200 x 100 mm (8 x 4 in) so estimating coverage is easy; you need 50 per sq m (42 per sq yd). Some are as thick as 65 mm (2½ in) or even 80 mm (3¼ in); other light-duty blocks are only 50 or 60 mm (2 or 2⅜ in) thick, and are intended for use as paths and patios rather than for driveways.

MORTAR AND CONCRETE

The raw materials used to make mortar and concrete are cement, aggregate of one kind or another, and various additives that improve the performance or ease of handling of the mix. It can be difficult to estimate materials accurately since they have to be ordered in large quantities for all but the smallest jobs, and waste costs money.

Cement is widely sold only in 50 kg (112 lb) bags, although some DIY superstores stock smaller and more manageable 25 or 40 kg (55 or 88 lb) packs. The mortar and concrete mix formulae below are based on the use of standard 50 kg bags.

Sand, both soft (for building or bricklaying) and sharp (for concreting) varieties, are sold either in bags or by volume. Bags – either 40 or 50 kg – are convenient for small jobs, but work out extremely expensive for large projects such as laying patios or concrete slabs. For these it is best to order by volume from a builders' supplier or transport company. The smallest quantity most will deliver is half a cubic metre, or about three-quarters of a ton. Remember that a cubic metre is some 30 per cent bigger than a cubic yard.

Aggregate is also sold bagged or loose by volume, and is graded according to the size of the particles they contain – fine if it will pass through a 5 mm (¼ in) sieve, and coarse otherwise. Coarse aggregates for concreting usually have a maximum stone diameter of 20 mm (⅞ in), although you can get 10 mm (⅜ in) aggregate for use in fine concrete. A cubic metre weighs nearly two tons, and is a surprisingly large heap when delivered.

DRY MIXED MATERIALS

DIY superstores and hardware stores stock small bags of dry, ready-mixed mortar and concrete – usually 25 or 40 kg sizes, occasionally in smaller packs down to 10 kg in size. The usual varieties include bricklaying mortar, rendering mix, and fine and coarse concrete. Use them where the scale of the job or where their convenience outweighs their comparatively high cost.

READY-MIXED CONCRETE

When ordering ready-mixed concrete, be sure to specify the volume of material you need, what it will be used for, when you want it, how you will handle the delivery and whether there is easy access to the delivery site. The supplier will then ensure that the appropriate

---

Below: *Split sandstone is a durable material and ideal for paving projects.*

mix for the job is delivered. To help you assess whether access is possible, most mixer trucks are up to 8 m (26 ft) long and 3 m (10 ft) wide, and can discharge their contents via a shute within about 3 m (10 ft) of the back of the truck.

MORTAR AND CONCRETE MIXES

For mortar, use table 1 to select the mix you need according to the job you are tackling, then use the formula for the mix as detailed under Mix types. For concrete, use table 2. The figures in column 3 of the concrete table are the amounts needed to make 1 cu m of concrete. Note that all mixes should be carefully proportioned by volume, using a bucket.

1: MORTAR MIXES

Use	Exposure	Mix
Walling	Moderate	Mix B soft
	Severe	Mix A soft
Pointing	Moderate	Mix A soft
	Severe	Mix C soft

MIX TYPES

Mix A
1:½:4 cement:lime:soft sand, or
1:3-4 cement:soft sand plus plasticiser, or
1:2½-3½ masonry cement:soft sand

Mix B
1:1:6 cement:lime:soft sand, or
1:5-6 cement:soft sand plus plasticiser, or
1:4-5 masonry cement:soft sand

Mix C
1:3 cement:soft sand

1 Mix the ingredients dry.

2 Form a central crater.

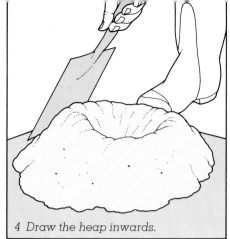

3 Pour in some water.

4 Draw the heap inwards.

5 Turn the mix thoroughly.

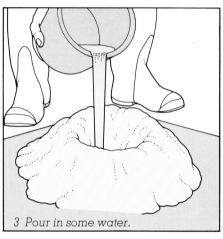

6 The right consistency is smooth and firm.

2: CONCRETE MIXES

Use	Proportion by volume		Amount per cu m	Yield per 50 kg bag of cement
GENERAL PURPOSE Most uses except foundations and exposed paving	Cement	1	6.4 bags	0.15 cu m
	Sharp sand	2	680 kg/0.45 cu m	
	20 mm aggregate	3	1,175 kg/0.67 cu m	
	OR All-in aggregate	4	1,855 kg/0.98 cu m	
FOUNDATIONS Strips, slabs and bases for precast paving	Cement	1	5.6 bags	0.18 cu m
	Sharp sand	2½	720 kg/0.5 cu m	
	20 mm aggregate	3½	1,165 kg/0.67 cu m	
	OR All-in aggregate	5	1,885 kg/1 cu m	
PAVING All exposed surfaces, all driveways	Cement	1	8 bags	0.12 cu m
	Sharp sand	1½	600 kg/0.42 cu m	
	20 mm aggregate	2½	1,200 kg/0.7 cu m	
	OR All-in aggregate	3	1,800 kg/0.95 cu m	

WORKING WITH CONCRETE

You may be using concrete to form foundation strips for garden walls, or to create a slab as a base for a garden structure. Start by clearing the site of surface vegetation – shrubs, weeds and the like. Then mark out the trench or slab shape with pegs and string, rope or hosepipe as appropriate, positioning your guidelines about 150 mm (6 in) away to allow you adequate room to position the formwork if this is needed to contain the concrete.

Next, excavate the site to the required depth. If you can re-use the soil elsewhere in the garden – as the base for a rockery, for example – pile it up neatly. Otherwise dump it in a skip.

You can now set the pegs that will

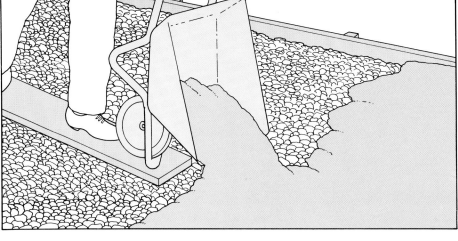

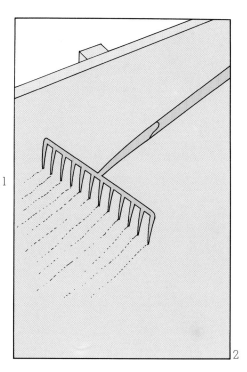

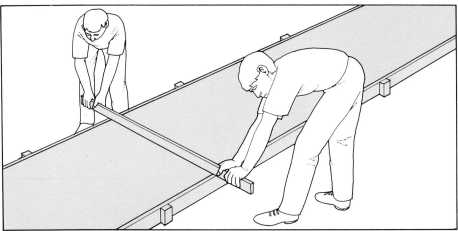

support the formwork in position. Use substantial timber – 50 mm (2 in) sq is ideal – and taper one end of the pegs to make them easier to drive in. Hammer them well into the subsoil, and use your spirit level or a water level to set their tops at the desired level for the foundation surface. Then nail the formwork planks to the pegs, and check that you have not disturbed them.

The next step is to put down a level of hardcore. Shovel it out evenly over the base of the excavation to a depth of around 100 mm (4 in) and tread or tamp it down thoroughly – a length of old fence post is an ideal tamping tool. Fill obvious gaps and hollows with smaller bits of broken brick or handfuls of aggregate.

You are now ready to lay the concrete. Simply tip it in (1), rake it out level (2) and, with a helper, tamp it down well with a stout beam long enough to span opposite sides of the formwork (3). Use a chopping action first of all to compact the concrete thoroughly, adding more concrete to any hollows that develop. Pay particular attention to the edges, tamping the concrete down firmly against the formwork. Then finish off with a sawing motion of the beam.

This will leave the concrete with a slightly rippled finish. If you want a smoother surface, you can work over the surface with a soft broom, the back of a clean shovel or a wooden plasterer's float. On large slabs this will mean forming a movable bridge from which you can reach all parts of the surface.

Left: *For ambitious projects, like this rock garden, you may need to hire some mechanical help to place the stones.*

The simplest way of making one is to use a ladder with planks laid on the rungs; rest the ladder on piles of bricks outside the formwork so the slight sagging as you kneel on it will not touch the fresh concrete surface.

Finally, as soon as the slab surface is hard enough not to be marked, cover it with polythene sheeting to prevent it from drying out too quickly (it will crack if it does). Weight the polythene down at the edges, and sprinkle sand across it to prevent it ballooning up and down in the breeze. Leave it on for about three days in colder climates; then remove it, and knock away the formwork. You can walk on it at this point, but you should wait a further five to seven days for the concrete to develop its full strength before starting building on it.

If you are laying a slab more than about 4 m (13 ft) across, you will have to include expansion joints to prevent the slab from cracking. You can incorporate these joints in one of two ways; whichever you choose depends on whether you are using ready-mixed

Below: *It is always worthwhile dry-laying paving stones before starting work in order to check where the cuts* (right) *will be needed.*

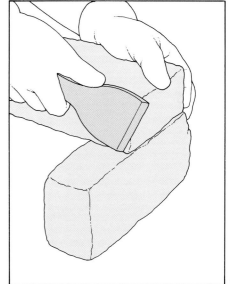

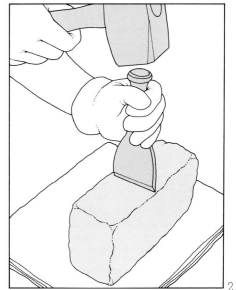

concrete or not. Aim to divide the slab up into two or three equal-sized bays, depending on its size.

If you are laying ready-mixed concrete, use hardboard filler strips running the full width and depth of the slab and held in place with blobs of concrete. The strips should finish level with the top of the formwork, and will remain in place once the slab is cast. If you are mixing your own concrete, simply create the bays with more form-work. Concrete one bay (or the two side bays if you have three) and leave to set; then remove the dividing formwork and fill the remaining bay, simply butting the new concrete up against the edge of the existing bays.

CUTTING BLOCKS AND SLABS

Whatever you are constructing, you are sure to need to cut blocks and slabs at some stage of the job. You need a sharp brick chisel or bolster and a club

hammer for most cutting work; an angle grinder can be useful for making cut-outs in paving slabs, and a hydraulic splitter will make light work of cutting block pavers, which can be hard to cut by hand.

To cut a natural or man-made stone block, lay it on a thin bed of sand or soil. Score it all round the desired cutting line with the tip of the chisel (1), then hold the blade upright on the cutting line and strike the chisel firmly with your club hammer (2). Repeat if neces-sary to split the block.

Use a similar technique to cut paving slabs, first scoring a line across the slab surface and then using the chisel and hammer to deepen the cut until the slab splits.

To operate a splitter, mark the desired cutting line on the face of the slab or block, place it on the base of the machine with the marked line beneath the blade, and pull down on the lever handle to 'guillotine' the block in two (3).

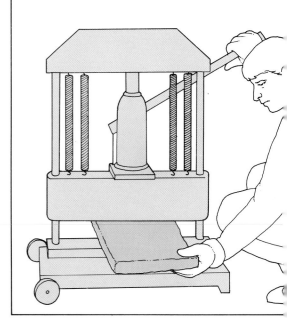

Additives Chemicals added to mortar and concrete mixes to improve their performance. The commonest include plasticisers, waterproofers and frostproofers.

Aggregate Sand or gravel added to cement to make mortar or concrete respectively. In Britain the term is normally used for all-in aggregate (also known as hoggin), a mixture of sand and gravel mixed with cement to make concrete. In South Africa, all-in aggregate refers to inferior material which should not be used.

Asphalt Tarmacadam.

Basketweave bond A pattern used when laying block pavers, consisting of pairs of blocks which are laid at right angles to adjacent pairs.

Batter frame A home-made timber building guide used in the construction of dry-stone walls to ensure an even backward slope to the wall face.

Baulk A stout length of timber.

Bedding plane The lines of natural stratification in sedimentary rocks.

Blinding layer A layer of sand used to cover a base of hardcore or crushed stone.

Block paver A reconstituted stone or concrete paving block designed to be dry-laid on a bed of sand in a variety of different interlocking patterns such as basket-weave, herringbone or running bond.

Bolster A steel chisel with a wide blade, used for cutting stone blocks and slabs in conjunction with a club hammer.

Bond The arrangement of blocks in a wall, designed to increase the wall's strength as well as to enhance its appearance.

Bricklaying trowel (mason's trowel) A broad-bladed tool used for spreading mortar when laying masonry or paving.

Builder's square A rough wooden triangle made up from sawn timber with sides in the ratio 3:4:5, and is used to check the squareness of masonry and concrete. Metal squares are used for fine work.

Carriage (trucking) costs The charge made for delivery of stone from a quarry or other supplier.

Cement The adhesive from which mortar and concrete are made. Portland cement is the commonest type. It is usually sold in 50 kg (112 lb) bags, although smaller sizes are also available.

Chisel An all-steel tool with a wedge-shaped or pointed cutter, made in a range of sizes and used to cut and shape masonry in conjunction with a club hammer.

Club hammer (lump hammer) A hammer with a heavy squared-off head and a short wooden handle, used to drive masonry chisels and similar tools.

Cobbles Small rounded pebbles set in mortar to form a path or other decorative surface detail.

Cold-roll macadam Macadam pre-packed in bags and specially formulated for laying when cold, unlike ordinary macadam which is laid hot.

Concrete A mixture of cement, sand and gravel (all-in aggregate) or crushed stone, used to cast foundations and slabs. It can be mixed by hand from dry ingredients, or ordered ready-mixed.

Coping stones Flat or ridged stones used to weatherproof the top of masonry walls. A coping can also be formed by a course of blocks laid on edge.

Coverband A stone spanning the width of a dry-stone wall, laid immediately before the coping stones.

Crazy paving (random paving) Paving consisting of irregularly-shaped pieces set on a mortar bed and pointed.

Crushed bark Shredded bark or wood chips used to discourage weed growth or to act as an informal path surface.

Damp-proof course (vapor barrier) A layer of impervious material incorporated in a masonry structure to prevent dampness rising into it from the ground.

Dressing The process of shaping the faces of a piece of quarried stone.

Flagstone (stone paver) A large square or rectangular slab of natural or man-made stone used for paving.

Formwork (shuttering) Timber used to support the edges of concrete slabs, paths etc while the concrete is placed. The boards making the formwork are nailed to stout pegs.

Foul water drain (sanitary sewer line) Underground pipework carrying water from household plumbing equipment.

Foundations Cast concrete strips or slabs laid to support walls and other stone garden structures.

Granite The commonest of the igneous stones, very dense and hard and widely used in the form of setts for paving.

Hardcore Crushed stone, broken brick, concrete etc used as an infill and support beneath concrete foundations on clay or other unstable ground.

Hearting (pinning or chinking) Small stones used to pack the heart of a dry-stone wall.

Herringbone bond A pattern used when laying block pavers. Each block is laid at 90° to its neighbour, and overlaps it by half the length of the block.

Hiring (renting) An alternative to buying tools and equipment, often more economical for seldom-used items.

Hoggin See Aggregate.

Honeycomb wall A supporting wall built with gaps between the building blocks to save on materials where the wall structure is subsequently hidden, as within a flight of steps.

Limestone A sedimentary stone consisting mainly of calcium carbonate, widely used for all sorts of garden stonework.

Masonry cement Ordinary Portland cement with added plasticiser.

Mortar A mixture of sand and cement with added plasticiser, used for building walls and bedding paving slabs.

mpa (mega pascals) Units to measure the compressive strength of concrete.

Paver (patio paver) A man-made hydraulically-pressed paving slab or block.

Pier A thickened section of masonry built at the ends of a wall and at intervals along its length for extra support.

Pointing The use of mortar to fill and finish the joints in walls and areas of rigid paving.

Preservative-treated timber (pressure-treated lumber) Wood that has been pre-treated with wood preservative.

Render coat (stucco coat) A coat of mortar applied to a masonry surface to weatherproof or decorate it.

Riven stone (splitface stone) Stone with a natural rough face, not dressed.

Running bond A pattern used when laying block pavers. The blocks are laid end to end throughout with joints in adjacent rows staggered, imitating stretcher-bond brickwork.

Sand Fine aggregate, graded as fine or soft sand used in mortar, or as coarse or sharp sand used in making concrete.

Sandstone A sedimentary stone consisting of fine or coarse particles of quartz bound together by a cement of other minerals, widely used for paving and walling projects.

Scutch holder A chisel-type tool consisting of a metal holder into which a variety of cutting edges - the scutches – are fitted; used when cutting stone to shape.

Sett A small square block of stone, usually granite, used for paving.

Shingle (pea gravel) Clean washed gravel, used as a path surface or for other decorative purposes.

Slate A metamorphic stone formed by the action of heat and pressure on clay, used mainly for paving and walling.

Stack bond A blocklaying bond used chiefly with square screen walling blocks.

Stretcher bond A building bond consisting of a single skin of walling blocks, overlapping each other by half their length in successive courses.

Tarmacadam (asphalt or black top) A mixture of crushed stone and tar used for paths and other surfaces.

Through stones Long stones running the whole width of a dry-stone wall.

Weep holes Unpointed gaps left between the blocks in retaining walls to allow drainage to occur through the wall.

INDEX